grill a christian

Answers to tough questions about Christianity, God and the Bible

Roger Carswell

Published by 10Publishing, a division of 10ofthose.com

Unit C
Tomlinson Road
Leyland
PR25 2DY

Email: info@10ofthose.com
Website: www.10ofthose.com

British Library Cataloguing in Publication Data. A catalogue record for
this book is available from the British Library

ISBN: 9781906173111

Printed in Denmark by Nørhaven

I dedicate this book to two groups of people:

First, to the tens of thousands of Christians across the world who are suffering because they asked questions, came to conclusions, and put their trust in Christ, but now suffer at the hands of people who oppress them wishing to suppress their message.

Secondly, to those who demonstrate their hatred for God by persecuting fellow human beings, simply because they follow Jesus. I pray that God would be merciful to you, helping you to ask the big questions as to who Jesus is, what has He done for you, and how He can bring you to know God.

Contents

Still a christian

Introduction

My work involves travelling around the UK, and different parts of the world, speaking to people about Jesus. Through this work I have become convinced that everyone is asking similar questions when it comes to Christianity, the Bible and Jesus. Whether it's the university professor or the drunk in the gutter – the same questions are asked. I am so convinced of this that I wondered for a while if the drunk in the gutter was also the university professor, only just at different times of the week!

Answering a question can be difficult, but asking a good question can often be harder still. This book is filled with good, genuine questions. They are all ones that I have been asked over the last number of years.

I have sought to answer them honestly, but not exhaustively. For ease of reading I have tried to answer with clarity and simplicity. However, I believe it is important to say that the answers found in this book originate from a much higher and greater source, in that my world view is definitely a Christian one, and I have gone to the Bible for answers. Why I have done this, you will see in some of the answers I have given.

Most of the answers that I have written are deliberately short, but you will see that some are much more detailed. These answers touch on other issues, and I hope will help the questioner who is wanting thorough answers to some questions. I suspect that this book will not be read from beginning to end, but rather be 'dipped into'. So for that reason, there is some repetition in some of the answers, which you may spot if you read a good number of the answers.

As things stand, I have six grandsons, with another grandchild on the way. Harry is the oldest but is still little more than a toddler. He loves playing Hide and Seek. However, this isn't the Hide and Seek that you and I are used to. Harry hasn't quite understood yet, that the idea of the game is that you're trying not to get found. For him the fun is getting found, which is usually followed by him getting tickled!

"Is Harry behind the TV?" releases a muted giggle from his hiding place behind the sofa!

"Or is he hiding behind the curtains?" He's now laughing so loud he can hardly contain himself.

"Or is he behind the sofa?" You barely have to get the word 'sofa' out and a squeak of high-pitched giggles escape from Harry's lungs and he runs out from his not-so-secret hiding place!

Harry wanted to be found, right from the beginning. In a similar way, God does not want to play Hide and Seek. He wants to play 'found'. God wants to introduce Himself to you. Asking questions to know more of who God is and what He has done is absolutely the right thing to do. I hope that this book will help you come to know God personally. The Bible teaches that if you seek Him, with all your heart, you will find Him.

I owe a great debt of gratitude to Janice Bowman, Jonathan Carswell, Michael Orr, Ossie Ross and Jean Smith for their helpful input.

Section 1

Questions about God

Who made God?

Nobody expects a dog to log on to the Internet and check out a national news website. This is not because the Internet cannot be understood, but because it is beyond a dog's understanding. Similarly, God is bigger than anything a human can fully comprehend. It is impossible to put God into a science lab and carry out experiments on Him.

God made men and women in His own image. The result is that we have the ability to love, think, reason, hate and to enjoy friendship. We were created by Him and must not fall into the trap of making God in our own image.

We are finite, God is infinite; we are limited, but God is not limited by space or by time; we were born and one day our bodies will die, but God has no beginning or end. He was not made by anyone or anything. Our minds cannot grasp that, just as they cannot understand the fact that there are innumerable stars in space, or billions of cells in our bodies. All that we know starts and finishes, but God had no beginning and will have no end. The Bible says of God that He is, 'the King of kings and Lord of lords, who alone is immortal and who lives in unapproachable light, whom no one has seen or can see. To him be honour and might forever.'[1] If we could fully understand and explain Him, He would not be God or we would not be human.

---

1.   1 Timothy 6 v. 15b - 16

The temptation is to reduce Almighty God to terms we can understand. This is the essence of idolatry. It is making God into our image, so that we have some control over Him. To give God a beginning is to create a being, who is like us. But God the Creator is greater than anything that He has created.

How do you know that there is a God?

The answer to this question affects the whole of our lives. As Christians we believe that God has revealed Himself to us in a number of ways, which I explain in the next chapter. God's revelation to us is the basic way of finding what we need to know about God.

One book of the Bible was specifically written to explain the Christian message. It is found in the New Testament part of the Bible, and is called Romans. Early on in the book we read, 'the basic reality of God is plain enough. Open your eyes and there it is! By taking a long and thoughtful look at what God has created, people have always been able to see what their eyes as such can't see: eternal power, for instance, and the mystery of his divine being. So nobody has a good excuse.'[2]

2. Romans 1 v. 19 - 20

The whole of the world shows the greatness of God. Each designer leaves his mark on his creation and this is true with God's creation of the world. From the intricacy of the human body to the tiniest molecule, from the largest mountain to the smallest cell, design needs a designer. Creation demands a creator.

The history of the world seems to point to an unfolding pattern that is heading in a direction, and has purpose. Considering all the different religions of the world, each seeking God with a desire to pray, leads to the conclusion that there is within human beings an awareness of someone to whom we owe allegiance, and of whom we are aware. Though I am deeply unhappy about Spiritualism, Yoga, Zen, Palmistry and so on, they nevertheless illustrate the eternal search for God that characterises us human beings.

Within us there is something that points to God. Universally, humans have a sense of morality. From childhood we know the difference between right and wrong. How do we know this difference? It is not only nurtured by society, but it is also part of our nature. The Bible teaches that God has put within us our conscience. His stamp is on us. It is interesting to note that when we face trouble, we soon find ourselves crying out to God. Sir Winston Churchill quipped "I have never seen an atheist in a lifeboat".

The question we have to ask then is this: do you truly believe in your heart that you are the result of a random chance? And, if that is true, what worth is there in life? Why do we love, long, and live for life at all? Such deep seated inward questions demonstrate that we are more than a conglomeration of chemicals covered in skin, and that there is a God who gave us life, and created us for a reason.

Yes, there is no scientific formula to prove God's existence, but there is plenty of evidence in and around us that demands an explanation. So, considering that Jesus claimed to be God, it is wise to look at Him and see if His claims were justified, especially as He said that He is the way to God.

Isn't faith a leap in the dark, and aren't the atheists really on the right track?

As atheism is placarded before us in bookshops and on the media, let me deal with this question fully.

I love the Hans Christian Anderson story, 'The Emperor's New Clothes'. I first came across it as a children's song. A couple of conniving conmen pretended to be tailors. Knowing the king's vanity about his clothes, they began a scheme to weave invisible garments. They told the king that only a fool could not actually see the clothes, and the king bought into it! He took off all his clothes and put on the invisible suit. Then he walked in a royal procession down the streets thinking he was showing off his magnificent clothes. At first the crowds exclaimed praise over what the king was wearing. No one dared expose the king's folly for fear of being thought a fool themselves. Then one little boy had the audacity to say, "Look at the king! Look at the king! He is altogether as naked as the day he was born!" The truth spread like wildfire, much to the chagrin of the king.

Recently, there has been a rise in fundamentalist atheism that is militant and 'in your face'. These 'new' atheists are parading something which is novel and telling us that if we can't see what they can, it is our own stupidity. They say that belief in God is akin to believing in Santa Claus.[3] These atheists regularly appear on radio and television expressing beliefs that either go unchallenged, or are questioned by rather quirky or ill-informed 'Christian' people. These 'no God for me' atheists, as the Bible depicts them, write books which through heavy promotion are best-sellers, advertised on the side of buses. They mock believers in colleges or universities and have accused anyone who disagrees with them as being 'ignorant'. They have portrayed themselves as the final authority on questions of morality, beliefs and what defines an intelligent person. They give the impression that anyone who knows anything about science cannot be a Christian.[4]

Atheism and its cousin Secularism have led to an attempt to banish Christianity from schools and the workplace. So we have seen cases of people being suspended from work for wearing a cross, for offering to pray with an elderly patient, or for sharing beliefs at work or in a classroom because it is deemed politically incorrect in our secular climate. The idea is imposed on us that Christian belief is not for today.

There is a desire to airbrush out of history the fact that it was scientists who believed in God - and believed that He created discoverable laws - who pioneered so many of the foundations

---

3. Richard Dawkins said, 'It is absolutely safe to say that, if you meet somebody who claims not to believe in evolution, that person is ignorant, stupid or insane (or wicked, but I'd rather not consider that).' Review of 'Blueprints: Solving the Mystery of Evolution', by Donald C Johanson and Maitland A Edey. New York Times, April 9, 1989

4. The chemist Louis Pasteur one of the main founders of microbiology, said "A little science estranges men from God, but much science leads them back to Him."

of scientific research: Isaac Newton, Johannes Kepler, Michael Faraday, Robert Boyle, Humphry Davey, Samuel Morse, Sir James Simpson and a vast list of others in more recent years.[5]

Yet it is amazing how easily exposed are atheistic arguments when they are intelligently challenged. It was the 200th anniversary of the birth of Charles Darwin, so on BBC Radio 5's late night phone-in programme, Richard Bacon had as his guest atheist, Professor Steve Jones of University College London. Though not as well known as Richard Dawkins, he comes across as less fanatical. He explained his belief that evolution made it unnecessary to believe in God. The callers simply accepted all that Steve Jones had to say until a guy called Vinny (Vinny Commons, a football coach from Southport), simply asked three questions, which totally silenced the professor and left Richard Bacon trying to cover for him. Frankly, it was embarrassing for the atheist who was found in the 'altogether'. The questions which left him floundering were:

1. You say you believe in the 'big bang'. What went bang?
2. How did life come from non-life?
3. You weren't there when the world came about, so how do you know what happened?

He couldn't bring himself to admit what Richard Dawkins had already done when speaking about evolution in a speech at Washington University in St. Louis, USA. He said "We don't need evidence. We know it to be true."[6]

Think about this: it is not hard to believe that there must always have been something, for something cannot come from nothing. So if there was never nothing, what was there before time and matter began?

This book is, as it were, a small voice crying out amidst the crowd,

---

5.   See www.answersingenesis.org for a substantial list of some famous scientists who believe that God brought the world into being or rules over all in an orderly and predictable way.

6.   World Magazine, 22nd March, 1997, p.10

that atheism is not what it seems and does not stand the test of cross-examination.

There is a basic dishonesty of atheism'[7]. If that sounds harsh, it is because in our sceptical age we are often taught that we cannot be absolutely sure about anything. There is an intense dislike of any appearance of certainty. Of course, in some ways scepticism is a good thing. We have grown increasingly sceptical of what politicians, journalists, philosophers, religious leaders and the like tell us; it is right to be questioning. That, though, does not mean that there can never be certainty.

Christians, people who have put their trust in Jesus Christ, have a knowledge of God that is certain. They not only believe - they know that God is real and that He has revealed Himself to humanity.

At the heart of atheism is human pride. Something in us all fights against there being Someone superior to ourselves. We want to be in control of all things. A true scientist, like anyone else, will admit their own weakness and fallibility. Carlos Frenk reflected, "We don't understand how a single star forms, yet we want to understand how 10 billion stars form."[8]

So, briefly, what is the evidence that God is real?

Everything we know about God is what He has revealed to us about Himself. He has made Himself known in many ways but here are listed some basic ones:

1. The wonder of creation.

To look at the petals of a beautiful flower, to consider the dexterity

---

7. The phrase is quoted from Professor Verna Wright, professor of rheumatology at Leeds University. He used it as a title for a lecture he was frequently asked to give in universities throughout the U.K.

8. Quoted by Robert Irion in 'Surveys scour the cosmic deep,' Science, Vol 303, 19 March 2004, p 1750

of the fingers of our hands, to hear the dawn birdsong, or the crashing waves of the ocean, cries out that behind design there must be a Designer, and creation must have its Creator.

Whether one looks through a telescope or a microscope there is evidence of careful, bold, intricate design. Gazing through the telescope one sees the vastness of billions of stars, billions of light years apart and through the microscope is the detail and intricacy of the DNA system and the billions of cells.

Sir Fred Hoyle wrote: "Now imagine 10^{50} blind persons (that's 100,000 billion, billion, billion, billion people; standing shoulder to shoulder, they would more than fill our entire planetary system) each with a scrambled Rubik's cube, and try to conceive of the chance of them all simultaneously arriving at the solved form. You then have the chance of arriving by random shuffling (random variation) of just one of the many biopolymers on which life depends. The notion that not only the biopolymers but the operation programme of a living cell could be arrived at by chance from a primordial soup here on earth is evidently nonsense of a high order."[9]

But muse on the positioning of planet earth in our solar system. Earth is perfectly positioned so that if our axis or distance from the sun was just minimally altered we would all either freeze or burn.

As someone expressed it, it is easier to believe that the Encyclopaedia Britannica came about as a result of an explosion in a printing factory than to believe that all of creation came about without a Maker. Chance would be a fine thing! The order, variety and extravagant beauty of our world reveal to us something of the nature of the creative God.

With our scientific advancement and the 'creation' of living forms

---

9. Sir Fred Hoyle and Chandra Wickramasinghe in 'Evolution from Space' (New York: Simon & Schuster, 1984), p176

within the laboratory, it has been suggested that we don't need God any more.

Someone told this imaginary story:

> A scientist got into an argument with God. "You're not the only creator," he declared. "I also can make a man."
>
> So God said, "Let's see you do it."
>
> The man walked over to some dirt. But God stopped him, and said, "Get your own dirt!"

Creating is making something out of nothing; manufacturing is making something out of something else! Only God can create.

2. The witness of our conscience.

Nobody is born an atheist. Richard Dawkins tells the story of how he tried to drill out of his daughter's consciousness the belief that there must be purpose in our existence (most of us would feel that that is brainwashing). God has placed eternity in the minds of men and women, so that we are at times overtaken with a sense of awe, wonder and the awareness of Someone greater than ourselves. We recognise the futility of life without God and whenever we are confronted by death something within us cries out that there must be more. Innately we are convinced of existence beyond the grave.

As well as this, within every human being there is a sense of right and wrong, of fair play and justice. One of the defining moments in the twentieth century was when the atheist Soviet Union President Khrushchev banged his shoe on the United Nations desk shouting, "It's not fair; it's not fair!"

If there is no God, there can be no absolute standard of morality or fair play, and yet morality, right and wrong, justice and fairness are written deep within our psyche. Where did they come from? Conscience is like a court of law built within us. It is willing to judge against us and find us guilty when we go against what we inwardly know to be right. We were created spiritual as well as physical beings, so we are made with an innate awareness of our responsibilities towards God and others.

Of course, conscience can be moulded by society, so a person's standards can become warped and twisted. In fact the Bible explains that this is exactly what has happened, and this ushered into our world chaos, calamity and cruelty.

The early chapters of the Book of Romans in the Bible are a powerful explanation of the Christian message. In the first chapter we read,

'The wrath of God is being revealed from heaven against all the godlessness and wickedness of men who suppress the truth by their wickedness, since what may be known about God is plain to them. For since the creation of the world God's invisible qualities – His eternal power and divine nature – have been clearly seen, being understood from what has been made, so that men are without excuse.'[10]

3. The Word of God, the Bible.

The Bible was written over a period of 1600 years by about 40 different authors from the Egyptian, Hebrew, Babylonian and Roman cultures. Yet there is total unity in thought and theme. There are 66 books in the Bible – 39 in the Old Testament, written before the birth of Jesus, and 27 in the New Testament, written after His birth. Some of these books are history, some poetry, others are prophecy, and a number are letters written originally to individuals or churches. They were finally bound together in one volume in recognition that God had spoken through these books to humanity as a whole.

The accuracy of the Bible needs to be explained away by atheists, if they won't believe it is the word of God. It has proved to be

10.   Romans 1 v. 18 - 22

archeologically and historically accurate, often to the surprise of those whose initial thought was that the Bible could not be correct. The Bible has pronounced on scientific issues thousands of years before scientists have 'discovered' what it had already said. For example:

- The oldest book in the Bible speaks of the earth's free floating in space thousands of years before modern science discovered the fact. '(God) stretches out the north over empty space; He hangs the earth on nothing.'[11]
- Long before Galileo talked about the earth being a globe, and when others talked about the earth being flat, the Bible spoke of the 'circle of the earth'.
- Thousands of years before medical science discovered the fact, the Bible taught that blood is the source of life and health. 'For the life of the flesh is in the blood …'[12]
- Centuries before oceanography the Bible taught that the ocean floor contains deep valleys and mountains. We read, 'Then the channels of the sea were seen, the foundations of the world were uncovered …' and Jonah said, 'I went down to the moorings of the mountains … yet You have brought up my life from the pit, O Lord, my God.'[13]
- Long before Ignaz Semmelweis (1818-1865) and Louis Pasteur (1822-1895) had established germ theories, the Bible taught sound rules of hygiene. For example, "When he who has a discharge is cleansed of his discharge, then he shall … wash his clothes, and bathe his body in running water; then he shall be clean."[14]

The Bible reveals to us:

who God is, and
who we are;
what God has done, and
what He wants us to do.

---

11.   Job 26 v. 7

12.   Leviticus 17 v. 11

13.   2 Samuel 22 v. 16 and Jonah 2 v. 6

14.   Leviticus 15 v. 13

Throughout, the Bible makes it clear that it is impossible for human beings to make their own way to God but that God has taken the initiative and reached down to us. It teaches that we are not saved by the good things we do. Rather, it is because of God's mercy that Jesus came into the world to be the substitute/ sacrifice who would pay for our sins. Dying on the cross, Jesus carried the can for all of us, so that we could find forgiveness, and reconciliation with God. This comes about when we put our trust in Jesus who died, was buried and rose again.

This contrasts with every other religion in the world. They each teach that we have to do certain things and become very good people to have any hope of being accepted by God.

But how do we know whether the Bible is true and is therefore the revelation of God?

Scores of times throughout the Bible we read that God speaks to reveal the future. These are not vague predictions such as one reads in a horoscope, but are very detailed and specific. (Incidentally, have you ever wondered why fortune tellers are not multi-millionaires, for they should be able to predict the lottery numbers successfully!) Bible prophets predict the fate of individuals, of cities and nations. There are numerous examples of these but to illustrate let us examine just one set of prophecies.

The whole of the Bible is about Jesus. The Old Testament anticipates His coming, His life, work, death, resurrection and His lasting influence. Over and over, there are detailed prophecies about Him, so that nobody would have an excuse if they missed His coming. The New Testament, written when there were hundreds of eye witnesses still living, describes Him, His work and teaching, and so demonstrates how this one solitary life fulfilled all the prophecies contained in what is really a Jewish book, the Old Testament.

Christians could not tamper with these prophecies because

they had been made centuries earlier and were contained in the Scriptures owned by the Jews. The prophets had foretold long before Jesus was born, and centuries before crucifixion was devised as a means of capital punishment, what would happen to the coming Messiah:

- He would be betrayed by a friend
- His back would be beaten until it was like a ploughed field
- He would be spat upon
- He would die a poor man's death but be buried in a rich man's grave
- He would be crucified between thieves
- He would have His hands and feet pierced
- He would have even His garments gambled for
- the bones of His body would be pulled apart but not a bone of His body would be broken
- even the words that Jesus' executioners would utter were predicted
- His body would not decay
- He would rise again from the dead.[15]

Now let the atheist explain who wrote in the present what would happen in the future, and get things so right!

If there is to be honesty among the atheists, they need to explain all these Bible prophecies. Who, but God, knows the future as well as the past? He has revealed Himself through His written word, the Bible.

When people begin to read the Bible, they find that God speaks with authority, convincing them of its authenticity.

4. The work of Christ.

There are many things about Jesus that I believe because they are recorded in the Bible. The Bible tells me that in Jesus, God

---

15. See Psalm 22, Isaiah 53, Zechariah 11 - 12, Psalm 41 v. 9, Psalm 16 v. 10

became flesh and made His dwelling among us. Therefore it is not difficult for me to accept that Jesus was born of a virgin: He came into this world as the God-man and therefore was born of deity and humanity. I cannot prove that Mary was a virgin at the time of the conception of Jesus, but I believe it.

Neither can I prove that Jesus fed thousands with a few loaves and fish. However, being God Himself who was walking on planet earth, it would be perfectly natural for Him to do this.

If Jesus really is God, His love would be such that He would want to heal the sick, and His power would be sufficient to do so! He would be able to calm a storm at sea by the word of His power, to cast out demons and to know the thoughts of those plotting against Him.

As the one who said of Himself, "I am the way, the truth and the life …," I would expect Him to be able to raise the dead and to conquer death by raising Himself from death.[16]

Intriguingly, the greatest of all miracles is Jesus' own resurrection from the dead and it is concerning this miracle that there is an overwhelming weight of historical evidence. Jesus did what no religious or political leader could - He conquered the grave.

There is no doubt that Jesus was dead. Professional Roman executioners were not going to be duped into pronouncing one of their crucified victims as dead unless they were certain He was demonstrably dead. Jesus had undergone the horrors of crucifixion as well as carrying the sin of the world on Himself. He gave up His own life, but to ensure that He really was dead the soldiers speared his side and noticed that blood and water poured out, as a sure sign that death had occurred. Then the body was taken down, tightly wrapped and laid in a tomb which was sealed.

---

16. See John 2 v. 19

The tomb was guarded to ensure that no one could tamper with the body. This was requested by the religious leaders of the day who knew that Jesus had said He would rise from the dead. But three days later the stone rolled away to reveal that the body of Jesus had gone and for the next forty days Jesus showed Himself risen and alive to literally hundreds of people, most of whom were still living when the record of the events was written. Of course, some were doubtful. Some, like the disciple Thomas, just did not believe, saying that unless he could put his fingers in the wounds of Jesus and his hand in His side, He would not be convinced. But when Jesus appeared before Thomas, he fell on his knees saying, "My Lord and my God".

The Jews and the Romans would have loved to have silenced the early followers of Jesus by taking them to the body of Jesus in the grave where He had been laid but they could not, for the body had gone!

Some have suggested that Jesus' body was stolen but who would have done that? Why would they do it? What would they have done with the body after that? No Jew would cremate a body and Jesus was already buried in a suitable place. How would the thieves get past the guards? Who could have acted like Jesus, with wounds in his hands, feet and side convincing even His closest disciples that He really was risen from the dead?

Some object saying that the disciples may have had some sort of hallucination, or maybe just falsified the story of Jesus rising to enhance who Jesus was perceived to be. But then why did the Jews and Romans not produce the body of Jesus, which they were guarding in the grave? Who convinced the sceptics like Thomas? Also, would the disciples, who were a fairly timid lot, be willing to die a martyr's death for what they knew to be untrue?

Further, to compound the evidence for Jesus' resurrection, remember that it was prophesied in the Old Testament long before Jesus was born. Jesus Himself repeatedly said that He would be crucified and on the third day rise again. The resurrection was recorded by Gospel writers, Matthew, Mark, Luke and John, who were in effect Jesus' biographers. Other Christian writers also wrote of His resurrection.

In addition to the testimony of Christian writers of the day, Roman and Jewish writers of that time also wrote about Jesus, His death and resurrection.

If atheists are going to come clean and be honest, they have to explain how Jesus rose from the dead.

5. Christian Conversion.

Christian belief is not merely academic. God has revealed Himself to the world at large, but He also makes Himself known to individuals and changes their lives. For two thousand years men and women have been radically transformed the moment they ask Jesus to become their Lord and Saviour. God has turned around the lives of men and women in such radical ways, that again the onus is on the atheists to explain what has happened. Conversion like this knows no parallel in any other religion or philosophy.

How else do you explain what happened to the self-seeking, materialistic, Yorkshire politician, William Wilberforce, who upon asking Jesus Christ to be His Lord and Saviour was so transformed that he gave himself unstintingly to the abolition of the slave trade and the founding of over 70 charities including what we know today as the RSPCA?

Who changed Lord Shaftesbury into 'the poor man's earl' devoting his life to the reform of the factory laws, children's working conditions and care of the underdog? His biography explains it was the moment of Christian conversion which made such a radical difference. It was the same for John Howard and Elizabeth Fry working to improve prison conditions, and for Dr. Barnardo and George Müller who cared for the orphans.

In more recent times, UVF terrorist David Hamilton was sentenced to life in prison for the crimes he had committed. An old lady started to pray for this 'no hoper'. Two and a half years into his prison sentence, served in the notorious Maze Prison in Northern Ireland, he read the title of a little gospel leaflet, which he mocked and threw away. But then, he strangely found that there was an inward pull to read the New Testament which was in his prison cell. He had already used many of the pages as cigarette paper, but he started reading and later that night, he who was guilty of crimes society regards as the worst, knelt by his bed and asked Jesus Christ to forgive him and to come to live in His life. That was all he did! Jesus did the rest. Now David works as a pastor of a church in the North of England. Can some honest atheist explain what happened?

Alison Stewart never knew a stable home life as child, and it was hardly surprising that eventually she would turn to drugs and prostitution to try to find fulfilment. Instead she found addiction, homelessness and abuse. She went on nine different drug rehabilitation courses all to no avail, as her life spiralled into increasing misery and meaninglessness. In a last desperate attempt to get out of the trap of addiction, she went to a Christian centre for drug addicts. After just three days a lady sat down with her and lovingly explained to her the gospel. Alison heard, for the first time in her life, of the God who loves her, who came into this world and died paying for her sin, and how the risen Jesus has the power to forgive and change her life. She prayed asking God to do just that, and in a moment she was set free from her addictions, and has found a new, purposeful life. Let the atheist explain that, please.

Professor Michael Clarkson was the professor of Veterinary Parasitology at Liverpool University. He came from an atheistic background in which his father had been a member of the Freethinkers. Yet as an undergraduate at university he had attended a lecture entitled 'The Impossibility of Agnosticism', in which he was challenged to read the Gospel of John. As he did so, he became convinced of the truth of Jesus and was to turn from all that was wrong in his life, and to turn to Jesus as His Lord, Saviour and Friend. Sixty years since then, despite many tough times in life, he has no doubt about the validity of the Christian message and the reality of a true and living God.

I once remember hearing Professor Norman Nevin, the professor emeritus in Medical Genetics at Queen's University, Belfast. As a pioneer scientist, whose discoveries concerning the value of folic acid have affected lives across the world, he explained to a huge crowd in Northern Ireland his absolute confidence that the Bible is totally reliable in all areas and the impact that Jesus has made on his life.[17] And this is the sort of man Dawkins calls idiotic!

What God has done for these four people - and millions like them - He is willing to do for you today. The Bible says that the fool has said in his or her heart that there is no God.[18] If you are willing to leave unbelief and your sin, then ask God to become your Lord and Saviour.

If that seems a step too far, perhaps you would at least read Matthew, Mark, Luke and John and allow the real Jesus to introduce Himself to you. He loves you as you are - but He loves you too much to leave you as you are.

Because Jesus has paid for sin on the cross, He will forgive you if you turn to Him. As Jesus has risen from the dead, He will give you the power and the desire to live for Him. Then, when it comes to eternity, you will find that the sin which would condemn you to hell has been dealt with. Heaven is not a reward, it is a gift for all who trust the Lord Jesus in a personal way. Hell is for those who refuse and reject the offer of new life in Jesus. The Bible teaches that God desires that none should perish and promises that if we seek for God we will find Him. In fact we will find that He has been patiently seeking for us.

---

17. His new book, 'Should Christians embace evolution?' is published by Inter-Varsity Press

18. Psalm 14 v. 1

Today, scientists are on a quest to find a grand unified field theory. They long to discover the 'glue' that brings quantum theory and astrophysics under one force or theory. Actually, it is God Himself who is the unified field they are looking for. There is a God-shaped gulf in every human being and, as it is God-shaped, only God can fill it. Only God can hold all things together, and through the finished work of Jesus who loved us and gave Himself for us on the cross, we can come to know Him now and for eternity.

It is not easy to turn away from an established position of atheism, but honesty requires it and God will help you if you are willing. Neither is it easy to carry on parading in the Emperor's new clothes.

What is God like?

My thoughts about God are no more valuable than anyone else's. All anyone can really know about God is what He Himself has revealed to us.

The Bible claims to be the written revelation of God. In it we read that there is only one God, and yet there are three Persons in the

Godhead: Father, Son and Holy Spirit. 'God is a spirit,'[19] and so cannot be touched or seen, but 'He appeared in a body....'[20] as God became a man and made His dwelling with us in the person of Jesus Christ.

Despite popular caricatures, we know that God is not like a genie who appears when an Aladdin's lamp is rubbed, nor a Santa Claus character, nor even an old man in the sky floating on a cloud! God is not human, and His thoughts are far higher than any of ours. The mediaeval scholar Anselm said, 'God is that, the greater than which cannot be conceived.'

The Bible also tells us that God is creative. We read how He conceived the world and brought it into being. All that He made was absolutely perfect.

We have all heard some news or received something in the post that has taken us by surprise. It came out of the blue; we weren't expecting it at all. This is an experience that God has never had. He has never exclaimed, "I didn't expect that!" The past, present and future are all in God's hand and control. Billions of human hours have been spent trying to understand the laws by which our world operates, yet God created and knows them all.

He is not only a creative God, but He is an all powerful (or omnipotent) God. He never grows tired, bored or disinterested. His power is infinite and He never runs out of it. God is omnipresent, so that it is impossible to escape from His presence. God is all knowing (omniscient). God never changes (immutable) and therefore is completely reliable. He is not affected by moods or impulses. He is eternal, with no beginning or end. He is beyond time.

God is absolutely holy and pure. He is more holy than we can ever even imagine or dream. He is so pure He cannot even look

---

19. John 4 v. 24

20. 1 Timothy 3 v. 16

on sinfulness. God's holiness is not only that He has not sinned, but that He cannot sin. Naturally we would never be able to approach Him because of our sinfulness.

God is absolutely just. He must punish sin. He cannot simply sweep our sin under the carpet or hide it away like a boy tidying up his room. If I were to burgle your house, and the police caught me, they shouldn't simply let me go saying, 'Naughty. Don't do that again.' This is neither fair nor right. The fact that most of us believe that crimes deserve punishment is in itself a reflection of the truth that God is just who must deal justly with our sin and rebellion. There is no injustice with God.

While this may seem very depressing for people who are sinful (which the Bible says is all of us) there is good news. As God is absolutely just, so He is also infinitely loving. In Jesus (God in human form) He has provided a way whereby we can have forgiveness. God's love and justice met together at the cross when Jesus died. God's love was demonstrated in that He (Jesus) died for us. Jesus paid the punishment for our sin, so that we might be forgiven and declared righteous in God's sight. Speaking in the Bible God says, 'Though your sins are like scarlet, I will make them as white as snow. Though they are red like crimson, I will make them as white as wool.'[21]

God is consistent in His judgements, as well as in other actions, thoughts and commands. Therefore He cannot contradict Himself. Neither can He act in a way that is contrary to His character. He cannot sin.

God is altogether awesome, yet it is possible for you and me to come to know God and for Him, through His Holy Spirit, to live within us and bring us to know Him forever.

---

21.   Isaiah 1 v. 18 NLT

What is meant by 'the Trinity'?

There is only one God. That is very clear throughout the Bible. Here are just two examples: in the first part of the Bible, the Old Testament, we read, 'Hear, O Israel, the Lord our God is one,'[22] Later, in the New Testament, we read, 'For there is one God and one mediator between God and men, the man Christ Jesus.'[23]

Whilst being one God, there is personality and multiplicity within the Godhead. Father, Son and Holy Spirit are equal, and each is God, yet they have distinct works. The Authorised version of the Bible says, 'For there are three who bear witness in heaven, the Father, the Word and the Holy Spirit; and these three are one.'[24]

God is far greater than anything human beings can ever understand. Nevertheless we have tried to explain and illustrate this concept of a 'three-in-one' God.

Some have used H_2O as an illustration. It is one compound, but can be found in the form of ice, water or vapour. Some have used human beings, who were created in the image of God, to illustrate God Himself – each individual is one, but comprises body, soul and spirit. St Patrick is supposed to have used the shamrock to illustrate the unity and yet three-fold aspect of one God. All these are helpful, but inadequate because God is infinite. God has revealed Himself in the Bible as one God, and also as the Father, Son and Holy Spirit. Each Person of the Trinity is described as having the qualities and attributes which only God has. In every great work of God, from the creation of the

22. Deuteronomy 6 v. 4

23. 1 Timothy 2 v. 5

24. 1 John 5 v. 7

world to the resurrection of Jesus Christ, and to the conversion of an individual, each Person of the Trinity is seen to be at work within that particular situation.

Christian people throughout the centuries have accepted this Bible teaching that there is one God who is triune in character.

Today, there are religions and new sects, which argue against this basic Bible belief. Muslims, Mormons and Jehovah's Witnesses, for example, detest the doctrine. But this is such a vital subject that listed below are some Bible verses which teach the doctrine of the triune nature of God, or deity of the Father, Son and Holy Spirit:

Genesis 1:26 (note the word 'our' and 'us')
Genesis 3:22 (note the word 'us')
Isaiah 9:6-7
Luke 4:18
Matthew 12:28
Matthew 28:18-19 (note the singular word 'name')
Luke 1:35
Luke 3:22
John 15:26
1 Corinthians 8:6
2 Corinthians 3:17 and 13:14
1 Timothy 3:16
Hebrews 9:14
1 Peter 3:18
1 John 5:6-7

Is it possible to have a God that both loves and judges: if God is a God of love, how can He judge too?

In reality judgement proves God's love. If God doesn't judge then He doesn't love. Let me explain. First, we are tempted to think of love as an emotional feeling of warmth or affection, but true love is far more than this. It is demonstrated in God, who is altogether loving. His love is pure and perfect. He cares about us, and about what happens to us. His love is so strong that He hates anything which spoils His lovely creation.

What kind of father would not care if his daughter was attacked? He'd be angry, and rightly so. It would be both natural and worthy to desire justice to be done. In the same way, God doesn't just let murderers get away with their sin. Because He cares He punishes all wrongdoing.

Not to judge would be immoral. Imagine the court scene: the judge walks in and sees the overwhelming evidence against the man who attacked the girl, and then the judge stands up and says he's a loving guy and so he will let the offender go free. That judge would have been unrighteous. Wrong deeds carry a penalty. God must punish our rebellion. That is why Jesus came to this earth and died as a substitute taking our punishment. He could do this as He was God and it is God whom we have offended. We will all face God one day and give an account for our lives. The Bible says, 'for the wages of sin is death, but the gift of God is eternal life, through Jesus Christ'.[25]

---

25.   Romans 6 v. 23

Do you believe God made the world?

The simple answer is 'yes', but let me explain why.

When you examine the Bible, reading it carefully, it gives great insight into the character of God, which is creative in a bigger way than we can ever imagine.

The media love to portray certain things as fact, like the age of the earth, for example, when actually they are merely protractions on the limited information available to us. These dates change from time to time depending on the latest information that has become available, thus reducing them to mere guesses. That is very different from 'fact'. The problem arises because we believe them to be true, because of how they are portrayed in the newspapers and on TV.

The Bible's first sentence tells us that God created the world. It is a truism that behind every creation is a creator. This stands whether it is the complex computer on which I am typing this book, the watch on my wrist, or the sprawled mix of colours my little grandson splatters on a page, that he calls a picture! They each have a creator. How then can we look at the world around us, whether an amazing sunset, a gushing waterfall, a tiny snowdrop, molecule or atom, or a gigantic galaxy of stars, and say there is no Creator behind it all? Are we really to conclude that it all happened by blind chance?

God spoke to nothing and created the world. He transformed nothing into something. He is the Creator and God of this universe and, therefore, deserves to be worshipped.

Is God bothered about our 'carbon-footprint'?

God, the creator of all things, is totally concerned with the world. The book of Genesis (in the Bible) describes how God intentionally and specifically designed and formed the world. After creating our world He paused and described it as 'good'. On completion of it all with the ultimate in creation, the first man and woman, God described it as 'very good'. God is concerned for His creation.

When creating humans He commanded them to take care of the earth and tend to its needs. However, Adam and Eve rejected God's plans and commands and lived for their own pleasure instead. In short, they sinned. As a result God cursed the earth, so that thorns were to grow and we humans would only live by the sweat of our brow. Farming and agriculture became hard work. Death entered the world, and the paradise that God made became a paradise lost.

As tenants of God's earth, we are to look after it. There is no excuse for abusing it. The Bible gives specific instructions concerning these issues. For example, it teaches that in war and in peace the land, vegetation and trees are to be cared for and protected. Animals are not to be cruelly treated. Each generation has a responsibility to care for itself and for future generations.

However, the overwhelming teaching of the Bible is that people matter to God much more than things, even things He has created. When a prophet in the Bible, called Jonah, was more concerned about a plant withering away than for the people living in the city of Nineveh, God spoke to him and said, 'You have been concerned about this vine, though you did not tend it or make it grow...But Nineveh has more than a hundred and twenty thousand people...Should I not be concerned about that great city?'[26] The Bible's teaching gives no place for animal rights activists who would kill or maim people for the sake of pursuing their own agenda.

Principles and trends need to be kept in line with God's priorities and truths. It cannot be right for parts of the world to so indulge themselves squandering the world's resources, while others suffer from sickness, starvation or want of basic needs. There has to be responsible and selfless use of the world's resources.

God shows His concern for the world to be righteous by promising one day to destroy this earth, with its corruption, disease and death, by fire. He will make a new heaven and a new earth. Meanwhile, this earth, cursed because of sin, can and should be a place where God is honoured by people who love and obey Him.

It is essential that we get our priorities right and our principles in order. Jesus Himself said, 'What good is it for a man to gain the whole world, yet forfeit his soul?'[27] It is proper that we look after the world, and everything in it, but we must first ensure our lives are in a right condition with God before we worry about other things.

---

26. Jonah 4 v. 10 - 11
27. Mark 8 v. 36

Section 2

Questions about the Bible

Why do you believe the Bible?

Before I started to read the Bible for myself I am not sure I did believe it. I had heard it read in Church, and even in school assemblies, but it wasn't until I actually opened it and read it for myself that its truth was revealed to me. I started in John's Gospel, which is a record of Jesus' life. It, or rather God through it, spoke to me as I read. It was as though Jesus walked off the pages and introduced Himself to me.

The Bible is a collection of sixty-six books, which are found in two sections, the Old and the New Testaments, bound together in one volume. As a whole it was written over a period of 1550 years by around 40 different authors from different backgrounds and situations. Despite this great variety and the long period in which it was written, there is total unity and consistency within it. Each author writes of humanity's ruin through sin, and God's remedy and rescue through Jesus. Jesus brings forgiveness, and the Holy Spirit brings new life to those who believe.

Imagine today trying to bring together a volume of over 40 authors who have written since 500 AD or so – what strongly varying ideas and contradictions there would be. This isn't the case with the Bible – there is no contradiction in thought or theme.

The first section in the Bible is the Old Testament. It looks forward to the coming of Jesus. The New Testament records Jesus' arrival on earth as a man, traces His life, death and resurrection, then His impact and ultimate reign on earth.

Time and again the Old Testament foretells, in minute and specific detail, the events of the future, which we then see in the New Testament. This is not done in a weird fortune-teller type of way, but rather pinpoints prophecies that we see come into reality, just as they were predicted, in the New Testament.

For example: execution by crucifixion was devised in around 300BC. However around 700BC Isaiah, a prophet, and before him around 1000BC, King David, both describe how One was coming who would die by crucifixion. Their description of the forthcoming events leave the reader who knows about Jesus, in no doubt that this is prophesying His death. They not only say how He will die, but also tell of the circumstances surrounding the events that day. They say His clothes would be gambled for; He would be sold for 30 pieces of silver; He would die a poor man's death in the prime of His life; be crucified between two thieves; buried in a rich man's tomb; His hands, feet and side would be pierced and yet His bones wouldn't be broken; that as He died He would take the sin of the world upon Himself; and that He would rise from the dead after three days.

These predictions are in so much detail, and there are so many of them, that this is no coincidence. God leaves nothing to chance. Instead God is in total control, and not subject to time, so He can, through the Bible, speak of what will happen. Only God can see the future and specifically and accurately write it down, as it will happen.

The Bible has God's imprint all over it. Like a crime scene that is smothered with the criminal's fingerprints, so it is with the Bible – it has God's prints throughout it.

Abraham Lincoln once said, 'I believe the Bible is the best gift

God has given to man. All the good from the Saviour of the world is communicated through this book'.

Do you believe everything which is in the Bible?

Having read the Bible through many times now, my answer is an unhesitating 'yes'. Let me explain why, because contrary to what people may think, it is not a blind trust.

There are different types of writings in the Bible. For example, there are parables, symbols, letters, narratives and dialogues from men and women, historical books, and even words spoken by the devil and people set against God. Despite the variety, all writings in the Bible are inspired by God and are profitable for teaching, rebuking, correcting and training in righteousness.[28] The historical books record what happened, sometimes good things, but other times, evil things. Poetry books in the Bible will have poetic expression, which are not intended to be taken literally. I have found that to let the Bible speak, with the most obvious interpretation being the one to take, allows God to use

28.   See 2 Timothy 3 v. 16

His word to bless the reader.

I have found that the very reading of the Bible leads one to believe it. There is something unique about it. God speaks to us through His word, and when we start reading it we learn more about Him, about ourselves and the importance of a relationship between Him and us.

Isn't the Bible full of contradictions?

As part of my work I am sometimes asked to go on radio phone-ins and discussion groups. I remember doing one such programme when a caller came through asking the very same question – doesn't the Bible contradict itself? The show's host answered the question for me when he asked the caller for an example. He couldn't. He was soon cut off and told to 'Get off the air and stop wasting our time!'

I became a Christian when I was 15, and since that time I have systematically read through the Bible many times. I have never once found a contradiction. It fits together like a perfectly interlocking jigsaw.

'An eye for an eye...'[29] and 'Turn the other cheek'[30] is often posed as a contradiction. In fact, both injunctions are valid. The first was given as an instruction by God to the nation of Israel who had been given the duty to uphold law and order and with that hand out a punishment that fitted the crime. They were forbidden from being either too severe, or too lax.

When Jesus added the words, 'Turn the other cheek', He wasn't speaking to a nation at that time, but rather to individuals, to you and to me. He was commanding that we don't take the law into our own hands, seeking revenge. Instead, we should be patient; turning the other cheek in order to show how good God is by being like Him. Turning the other cheek is not the easy option, but rather the right one, letting the authorities that God has given us to be responsible for the enforcement of the law.

If we take either statement/verse out of context it would appear that the Bible contradicts itself, but to do that would not be fair or accurate. The Bible is too important to play games with. I encourage you to read it for yourself – unlike the caller to the radio show!

29.   Exodus 21 v. 24
30.   Matthew 5 v. 38 - 40

How can we believe an old book that was written by believers years after the event?

Luke begins his account of the life of Jesus with these words: 'Many people have written accounts about the events that took place among us, just as they were handed down to us by those who from the first were eye witnesses and servants of the word. Therefore, since I myself have carefully investigated everything from the beginning it seemed good also to me to write an orderly account for you'.

Despite the accusations to the contrary, the New Testament documents are historical, so much so that they are like historical gold dust. Let me explain: how do we know anything about history – for example, Julius Ceasar? The answer is, through documents as well as archaeological and circumstantial evidence. The Gospel accounts in the New Testament are a collection of historical documents.

First, the writers were conscious that they were recording history. See how they record descriptions of scenes, place names, time of day and year, officials in Rome, festivals and Jewish authorities. This is not make-believe. The New Testament documents agree with what we know from historical accounts of the world at the time.

Secondly, examine the time scale. The documents were written within living memory of the events – all before 90AD. One archaeologist, WF Bright, stated 'the period is too slight to permit any appreciable corruption'. Remember too that the culture of that day included written memorisation which was the almost universal method of education. The incidents in the life of Jesus, as well as His teaching, could be remembered and recorded easily.

Thirdly, consider the writers. These were people who either knew Jesus or had based their gospel on the eyewitness accounts of Jesus' life. In the end some of them were killed for their beliefs about Jesus that were contained in their writings. Wouldn't they have been quick to deny their stories upon threat of death? I wonder whether the real issue with people who do not accept the historical reliability of the New Testament is that if they do they have to deal with the claims of the authentic Jesus.

Where would you recommend me to start reading the Bible?

Don't be put off the Bible simply because you don't know where to start. This doesn't have to be the case, and that's why this question is such a good one to ask.

I would suggest reading a section or book called John's Gospel. It is an eyewitness account of Jesus' life. The whole of the Bible is about Jesus and points to Him. Therefore, to read about

Him, understand Him and get to know Him is so central to the Christian faith that reading about Him is critical.

The Book of John is in the second section of the Bible, the New Testament. If you're unsure where to find it there is always an index at the beginning of the Bible. After reading John, I would advise reading the other three accounts of Jesus' life, Matthew, Mark and Luke.

Before reading the Bible, God's word, I suggest you ask Him to make Himself known to you as you read. As we have said before, God wants to reveal Himself to us. If you ask Him, He will hear you, and answer.

Hasn't science disproved the Bible?

Over recent years many have sought to make science and God mutually exclusive. They say that belief in God is old fashioned folklore. Nothing could be further from the truth. There is no credibility in this argument. It really is a myth. History shows that science and theism go hand in hand.

First, so many of the fathers of modern science - Galileo, Newton,

Farraday, Bacon, Kepler and more - were all people who believed in God. The Bible teaches that God is orderly and rational. Therefore, it follows that His creation is too. There are laws that can be tested, so that the world's orderliness can be studied. Of course, there are aspects to creation which cannot be measured, such as the beauty of our world and its ability to inspire awe and wonder. This in itself speaks of a Creator who is more than just an engineer! Essentially science comes from a belief in God.

The trouble is that we have cloaked the scientist with a mantle of infallibility, but a true scientist is known by his or her confession of ignorance. For example, Johannes Kepler, who discovered that planetary orbits are elliptical, reflected, 'O God, I am thinking Thy thoughts after Thee.' Isaac Newton said: 'I do not know what I may appear to the world, but to myself I seem to have been only like a boy playing on the sea-shore, and diverting myself in now and then finding a smoother pebble or a prettier shell than ordinary, whilst the great ocean of truth lay all undiscovered before me.' The inventor Thomas Edison once stated, 'I do not know one millionth part of one per cent about anything.'

Edward Jenner, the discoverer of the benefits of vaccination, said, 'I do not wonder that men are grateful to me, but I am surprised that they do not feel gratitude to God for thus making me a medium of good.'

After all, scientists cannot explain the source of kindness, love, beauty, friendship or fairness. They cannot say where we are going, or why it is that humankind universally demonstrates a spiritual dimension and a desire to worship.

A second myth is that Christians belittle science. Actually, Christians believe that science is good. It explains much of the world and helps us in medicine and technology as well as exploration. The Bible tells us to be good stewards of the world and to do so we will want to understand it.

So why is there a problem? The reason is that too often God has been used to explain the inexplicable – the God of the gaps. When things like the weather are beyond our control we speak of an 'act of God', but as soon as science can explain these things the need for God disappears. This is false reasoning. Being able to describe how something works doesn't take away the fact of a Creator and Sustainer.

Imagine you walk along the street and you come across a watch on the floor. You have no idea how it works, but you are happy to deduce that someone made it and put it there. What happens if you slowly learn how it works? Would you then say it had no maker? Of course not!

Science explains how things work in normal circumstances. This doesn't rid us of God; rather it shows us His greatness.

Science does not contradict the Bible, nor does the Bible contradict science. There are, however, scientific theories (rather than proven facts) and misguided biblical interpretations that may give the impression that there are contradictions. Perhaps limited knowledge leads to limited theories upon which many feel they can build a case and a life that excuses them from trust in God.

In all the world there is the seal of a great and amazing Creator of such marvellous things. I once saw a cartoon that expresses the wonder of the beauty of creation. It showed two monks surveying some marvellous scenery in the distance. One was saying to the other, 'I like his use of green in the bottom left-hand corner!' Nature testifies to the glory of God. It is reasonable to believe that behind designs there must be a Designer, behind something made there must be a Maker, behind creation there must be a Creator.

But the sceptic will also question the miracles. Again, though, if God is truly God He is well able to intervene, even if the result does not act in accordance with the usual observable laws of nature. Here is a clue to overcoming what has been a problem to some. A scientist is limited in being able to explain only what he actually sees. If God is taken into account, the explanation and outcome may be very different.

For example, given a piece of bread and asked to describe how it was made, a scientist would naturally detail how the seed was planted in the earth, its growth, harvesting, grinding, mixing with other ingredients and finally its baking in the oven. Of course, that would be fine, unless, that is, something remarkably exceptional had happened. Suppose, instead, the particular piece of bread under examination was one that had been picked up after Jesus had taken five loaves and two fishes, given thanks, then broken and distributed them to feed the five thousand, as described in Matthew chapter 14, verses 13 to 21. We read that twelve baskets of leftovers were gathered. If the piece of bread in question was one of these fragments, or from the incident a little later when Jesus fed four thousand with seven loaves and a few fish (read Matthew 15:29-39), the scientist would have been wrong in his analysis and description, because he failed to take into account the supernatural hand of God.

The scientist would make a similar and understandable mistake if he described the birth, growth, catching and grilling of the fish, if in fact this too was the product of miraculous and instantaneous multiplication by Jesus.

Or again, suppose wine was given to a professional wine-taster or a scientist to describe its country of origin and vintage. As he swilled it round in the glass, smelled and tasted it, he could perhaps describe this mature-tasting drink, perhaps even locating its country of origin and pinpointing one of the finest vineyards in that land. However, this time, far from being the natural product of grapes that had undergone years of fermentation, it was made in an instant. Jesus was attending a wedding feast at Cana in Galilee, as described in John 2:1–11. The wine ran out, but Jesus commanded that six large earthenware pots be filled with water.

As the chief steward tasted the drink, he found it was the best of wine. Knowledge of the presence of the One who created it would change the whole outlook on the wine itself. It was made in an instant rather than the long process that appeared to be the more obvious method.

If the Bible is as it claims to be, the word of God, then we would expect to read of the works of God. If these were within the realm of normal human experience then one would rightly question whether they were a demonstration of God or merely of humans. It is surely reasonable to expect God to work in ways that are beyond human comprehension. This does not disprove the Bible but demonstrates the infinity of God and the limitations of our finite minds and scientific pursuit.

Can't you prove anything you want from the Bible?

Like any piece of literature, yes, you can, if you twist, distort and misquote it. Sadly there are people who do that with the Bible, as there were in Jesus' day. If you take a sentence or passage out of context you can make the Bible say what you would like it to, to fit your argument or way of living. This is dishonest and something which the Bible itself warns against.

When, however, the Bible is read as a whole, in context, openly and honestly, its message is very clear. In inspiring the Bible, God was not aiming to confuse or mislead the reader. His Word is there to reveal Himself to humans.

Reading the Bible gives us an opportunity to understand God's plan, His purpose for our lives, and the way He wants us to live. Ignoring the Bible, even distorting it or misapplying it, is to neglect the treasure trove from God, which tells us about life's big issues.

Why don't we read about dinosaurs in the Bible?

I have often been asked this intriguing question.

The Bible doesn't speak of 'dinosaurs', but neither does it speak of the dodo or even cats. This could be taken further: the Bible doesn't talk about many things found in life today – wi-fi hotspots, cars or iPods.

However, just because the Bible doesn't specifically talk about dinosaurs or any of these other items doesn't mean they don't or didn't exist. The non-mentioning of them is not a good argument for their non-existence. The Bible is not an encyclopaedia, or zoological catalogue.

Having said that, there is mention in the Bible of animals with names like leviathan and behemoth,[31] which we read were huge creatures, and some have speculated that maybe they were dinosaurs. Whether or not they were does not alter the accuracy of the Scripture.

Hasn't Dan Brown proved the Bible to just be a legend?

It is not easy to write an international number one best seller. Dan Brown's 'The Da Vinci Code' has all the right ingredients. It's a blockbuster fiction book, and film, a gripping thriller, with sexual intrigue and some interesting characters. It also rewrites the Christian message, and that in itself appeals to many people.

31.　Eg Psalm 104 v. 26 or Job 40 v. 15

Before the story begins, there is a page marked 'Fact', which tells the reader that 'All descriptions of artwork, architecture, documents, and secret rituals in this novel are accurate.' But, that sentence is itself fiction. Eight times in the book, the author writes that 'art historians', 'religious historians' or 'all academics' believe something or other. Each time they appear to be fact, but Dan Brown is writing fiction.

Who are these historians? What qualifications and positions do they hold? What proportion of historians actually agree with what Brown writes? Brown is simply writing his fictional novel, so doesn't tell us names.

David Shugarts in his book 'Secrets of The Code' says that he has listed from Brown's book 69 factual errors, eight of which are trivial, but 61 are significant errors of fact or history. That is one error every seven and a half pages. It means that two out of three of Dan Brown's interesting 'facts' are actually untrue! If I was Dan Brown I would be seriously embarrassed about this! These errors would hardly matter, except they are on issues concerning God, Jesus, and the Bible. Nobody can afford to be gullible or fooled about such matters, for how a person responds to Jesus Christ matters for eternity.

Dan Brown says, for example, that the Bible has 'evolved through countless translations, additions, and revisions'. We have about 5,700 early Greek New Testament manuscripts, which is far more than of any other ancient book. It means that we can be sure that we have the original texts. Translations are all about trying to provide, from the original languages, an up-to-date translation of those documents. That there are many translations in print today is evidence of the integrity of the translators who revise their work to try to guarantee accuracy.

God is a person, but whether God is male or female was not an issue for Bible writers, as it is for Dan Brown. We read in the Bible of God's 'Shekinah' glory: but that is not a female-equal to God, but rather God's glory seen in the Temple. These things are very clear in the Bible, and one wonders why Dan Brown thinks his readers are so gullible.

The Da Vinci Code says there were originally over 80 Gospels (biographies of Jesus). But again, this is not true. In the first 300 years after Jesus, there were about 15 biographies, four of which are in the New Testament part of the Bible. There were six other fragments and a few legendary stories of Jesus' childhood. However, the point about Matthew and John is that they were eye witnesses, and Mark and Luke based their writing on eye-witness testimony. Later legends are only what they claim to be – legends.

The Dead Sea Scrolls were first found in 1947, with various scrolls discovered up until 1956. Dan Brown says they were discovered in 1950 and that the Roman Catholic Church suppressed them because they contained potentially damaging information about Jesus and Christianity. However, most were written before the time of Jesus, and only some in the first century AD. They were delayed in publication because it is difficult to piece together tiny fragments, but they are available to be read today, and do not mention Christianity. As for Constantine commissioning a new Bible, the New Testament was established 100 years before Constantine! And he didn't change the Christian Sabbath from Saturday to Sunday. Actually, we read in the Bible that Jesus' earliest followers began worshipping on Sunday to commemorate Jesus, who had died for their sin on the cross and then risen again on the first day of the week, Sunday.

In the New Testament alone there are about 500 verses where it is taken for granted that Jesus is Himself God. God took on Himself human flesh, so that Jesus is both fully God and fully human. It was not decided at the Council of Nicea that Jesus was God, but rather when people then, like Brown today, questioned it, Christian leaders gathered to address the wrong teaching. The vote was 316 (over 99%) to 2 (less than 1%) but Brown calls that a relatively close vote!

The Da Vinci Code says that Jesus and Mary Magdalene (who is only mentioned 3 or 4 times in the Bible) were married, and had a child. Clearly Dan Brown is writing fantasy. No ancient document ever says that Jesus was married. The idea of Jesus having a child was first written 800 years after Jesus. "Would you trust the inhabitants of Planet Earth 2800AD to 'discover' new information about you?" Neither was Mary Magdalene from the tribe of Benjamin, and that wasn't the royal tribe anyway! Brown refers to The Knights Templar finding secret documents under the Temple in Jerusalem which contain forbidden information about Jesus. However, nobody else knows of these documents, and Brown hasn't been able to produce them!

Dan Brown loves secret societies. The Priory of Sion is supposed to guard the secrets of the Knights Templar and has been headed up by people like Isaac Newton and Leonardo da Vinci. However, the man who wrote about this first, Pierre Plantard, testified under oath in 1993 that he had made up the whole thing.

Why, when so many writers have shown Brown to be deeply and repeatedly flawed, does he stand by what he said? Like many earlier books, he gives his readers excuses for not treating Jesus Christ seriously. It is all too easy to invent conspiracy theories. The Bible warns us not to follow cunningly devised myths, but as Napoleon is supposed to have said, 'It is amazing what people will believe as long as it is not in the Bible!' There is within all human beings an antagonism to God, because we are born with a sinful nature.

Though the Church has sometimes been guilty of authoritarianism, Bible Christianity has no place for such misuse of power. Christianity is not anti-women; rather Jesus by His deeds and words, liberated women. Repeatedly, the Bible proclaims Jesus to be divine.

The death and resurrection of Jesus never feature in The Da Vinci Code, but they are central to the Christian message. Christianity is not good advice, but good news. Our wrongdoing is deadly serious because it cuts us off from God and brings condemnation on us. Jesus came to deal with our sin. When Jesus hung on the cross, He was paying the penalty for our sin. God's just anger against our rebellion was laid on Jesus, who died as the substitute for us. Having carried our sin, Jesus rose from the dead, and is Lord of all.

What a difference there is between the real Jesus we read about in the Bible and the smoke and mirrors of Dan Brown's story. Brown wrongly says, 'Most people keep a chronicle of ministry'. Eyewitnesses, however, did record that Jesus was born, lived, taught, ministered and 'that Jesus died for our sins … that He was buried …that He was raised on the third day according to the Scriptures'.[32]

You and I would never undergo something as serious as medical treatment, or invest our life's savings, without having compete trust in the doctors or financial advisors. Therefore, read Matthew, Mark, Luke or John for yourself. Be introduced to the real Jesus. Ask Him to become your Lord, Saviour and Friend forever. It is wrong to try to rewrite history, to devise a Jesus who makes no claims on our lives and has no challenge, even if it leads to a book becoming a money-spinning best seller. Most important is to know that you are in a right relationship with God, through Jesus who loves us and came into the world for us. There is nothing secret about that.

---

32.   1 Corinthians 15 v. 3-4

Where did Cain get his wife?

This question makes me laugh! It is one that has been asked for years, usually in the pub, or the school common room or staff canteen. It's asked by people who haven't read the Bible (because the answer is clear in the first couple of pages) and by asking it they are really making a statement, 'I haven't read the Bible and don't believe it, and this question is my excuse.'

It is quite sad that that is the case. My fear in answering this question is that the people asking this particular one don't really want to take God's Word seriously.

In the first book of the Bible, Genesis, we read that Adam and Eve, after having two sons, Cain and Abel, also had a son called Seth. As we read on we are told that Adam also had 'many other sons and daughters…'[33]

Cain therefore married one of his sisters. Marriage between such close family relations is unacceptable and problematic for us today. Professor Verna Wright of Leeds University explained, 'At the beginning of the human race this was all right. Later, when inter-marriage could be dangerous because of the likelihood of disease-producing recessive genes manifesting themselves, the Bible laid down clear guidelines about this – a remarkable provision when the science of genetics was unknown.'

---

33. Genesis 5 v. 4

Isn't God different in the Old and New Testaments?

We have already discussed in previous chapters that the Old and New Testaments are completely consistent with each other. They interlock and complement each other perfectly.

God is utterly consistent and unchanging through all sorts of situations and trends. When the two Testaments are read as they were intended, they reveal the same God who is rich in mercy, but will not let sin go unpunished. Whether we are reading the Old or the New Testament we see the same characteristics of God being portrayed.

The God of the Old and New Testaments, the God of the Bible, is holy, powerful and just. He is also loving, full of love that we don't deserve, and will fulfil His purposes.

Didn't God sanction war in the Old Testament?

To understand this answer correctly, and in context, we must understand that God hates wrongdoing. He cannot tolerate it. The Bible's word for it is 'sin'.

In all cases in the Bible where God allows or commands life to be taken, it is as a consequence of a people's sinfulness. Without exception this is true. God is holy, and pure. All sin is abhorrent to Him. In the very beginning God warned Adam and Eve, the first humans, that if they disobeyed Him, they would 'surely die.'[34] They did just that, and true to God's word, death entered the world.

So does God counter wrong with another wrong? No, because although death is a dreadful thing, God at times commands people to be put to death, or forfeit their life, not for revenge or out of inappropriate anger but because God is just and sin cannot continue unpunished. God, the Giver of life, and the One who takes it away, will at times end a life to prevent the prolonging of wickedness. This can happen to nations, cities and individuals.

It would be natural then to feel that every individual deserves such condemnation. But the wonderful news is that God has acted to put away our sin. Sin brings death. The Bible says, 'that without the shedding of blood there can be no forgiveness of sin.'[35] Out of love for us, Jesus has come to die as a sacrifice for our sin. The Bible says that 'Jesus came only once and for all, sacrificing Himself... He was offered as a sacrifice once to take

34. Genesis 2 v. 17

35. Hebrews 9 v. 22

away the sins of all time. He came at just the right time to take away the sins of many people…'[36]

You and I can have freedom from sin - and the punishment it deserves - through the costly death of Jesus. He has exchanged places with us – our guilt was taken from us and laid on Him so that we may be given a 'non-guilty' verdict. The question is will we accept this offer by receiving Jesus into our lives?

Aren't there genocides in the Bible?

God is the author and the giver of life. His character is creative, holy, loving and just. Strangely we, who are the ultimate in all of God's creation, have deliberately defied Him. There have been times in history when nations have become so perverse in their rebellion that all boundaries and restraint have been banished. (Sadly, we have seen this recur in the 21st century as old barbaric acts have revisited us). The Bible, which contains much history, has recorded some of these periods, when child sacrifice became the norm, along with gross brutality, beheadings, crucifixion as well as paedophilia and sexual perversions. There were occasions in the Bible when acting in justice God instructed that the continuation and spread of evil should be stopped. He

36. Hebrews 9 v. 26b – 28a (NCV)

commanded that the people be put to death, and so sent to a higher court to be judged, i.e. in death they would meet their Maker in judgement.

Though these times were very rare, they are reminders that we cannot mess with God forever. It is worth remembering though, that even in judgement, there is mercy. Mercy, in that God was 'drawing a line' under a nation so that succeeding generations would not continue in perpetuating wickedness. And mercy, where God rescued people from judgement, even at the last moment, when there was true repentance. The dramatic story of the prostitute Rahab in Joshua chapters 2 and 6 is an example of this. She was even to become an ancestor of Jesus, who is the ultimate example of rescuing men and women who turn from their sin and trust Him.

The word 'genocide' inevitably stirs up emotions of anger and cries for justice. And we rightly cry for peace and reconciliation. However, in the Bible there is nothing gratuitous about God judging nations for their outright wrongdoing. God is described consistently in all the Bible as patient and kind, whose love is such that He does not want anyone to perish but longs that all should come to know Him. But just as in recent years we have known such outrageously wicked acts whether in New York, London, Paris, Beirut, Moscow or Bali, that when those planning it are 'taken out' we sigh with relief, so too there have been times when God has put an end to nations who have become characterised by gross wickedness. God is love, but He is also just. And love is not true if it is not just.

Doesn't the Bible forbid eating prawns?

The Bible has various types of writings: poetry, history, prophecy, letters, biography, and law. God gave laws to His people who were living in a theocratic (God-governed) nation. Some of these laws concerned religious ceremony, others religious observance, and some were simply rules governing social actions and personal activity. There were good reasons of hygiene for food such as prawns or pork to be forbidden, though there was religious symbolism too. God was demonstrating that His people, the Israelites, should live differently to nations around them. That difference was to be shown in several different but obvious ways.

However, it was made clear in the New Testament to God's people, namely all who have put their trust in Christ, that such limited rules had served their purpose and no longer applied. In Acts 10 God spoke to Peter and said he was to eat the meat of animals that Peter was objecting to saying they were 'unclean'. "Do not call something unclean if God has made it clean".

God has given some instructions, contained in our Bible, that served a comparatively short period of time only. Later, the Bible explained why they have now been put to one side, although there remain spiritual principles from these rules, which are helpful to people of all times.

I remember hearing a well-known politician ridiculing the Bible on BBC's 'Question Time.' She raised the issue of prawns! Actually, she was really demonstrating her ignorance of the Bible, and clearly had not carried on reading but stopped short.

What is the main message of the Bible?

As we have already seen, the Bible contains a variety of different genres of writings, penned by different people at different times. However, its message is consistent and reliable.

I hardly dare summarise its message, but the main themes are dominant:

God created a perfect world into which He placed human beings. They were to care for God's creation and bring pleasure to Him by being with Him. They were to follow His rules and in doing so they would be prosperous and happy.

From the very beginning, however, humans wanted to live their own way. Adam and Eve, the first humans, rebelled and turned their back on God – they wanted to live for themselves. They disobeyed God. We do the same today. The Bible says, 'All have sinned and fall short of the glory of God.'[37]

Because God is just, He cannot allow sin and rebellion to go unpunished. Like a judge in a courtroom He cannot turn a blind eye to the wrong that has been done. The Bible says that the punishment for sin must be eternal death, which is separation from Himself. While God is just He also equally loves. He wants to rescue us from the judgement we deserve. So the Bible says, that 'God demonstrates his own love for us in this: while we were still sinners, Jesus died for us'.[38]

This is why Jesus came to earth – He came to die. And when

37. Romans 3 v. 23

38. Romans 5 v. 8

He died, on an awful Roman cross, He carried the judgement of all the sins that you and I have ever committed. He took the judgement sentence that we deserve upon Himself so that we could be declared innocent.

Therefore the Bible goes on to say, 'If you confess with your mouth 'Jesus is Lord' and believe in your heart that God raised him from the dead, you will be saved'.[39]

The Bible is one big rescue story. God is rescuing us, through Jesus, to bring us back into a relationship with Him.

The Bible describes the new life that a Christian will experience in life, through death and into eternity. It also tells how God will ultimately bring all things under His rule as Jesus reigns in His rightful position as Lord of all.

39.   Romans 10 v. 9

Section 3

Questions about Jesus

Is the account of Jesus reliable?

How can we be sure that events that took place such a long time ago were recorded accurately as well as their record being preserved without distortions to it? The integrity and purity of any old manuscript depends on, and can be proved by, the number of documented manuscripts and fragments of manuscripts that still exist.

Classic texts from history, like those of Plato, Caesar, and even Homer's Iliad, that we trust and accept without hesitation, all have ancient manuscripts to show their authenticity. The New Testament alone has 24,000.

The account of Jesus can be trusted because its record is extensive, accurate and pure. The historians, who largely are not Christians, have found and verified the documents. There is no question that the gospel accounts of Jesus are true and reliable.

Respected theologian FF Bruce commented, 'There is no body of ancient literature in the world which enjoys such a wealth of good textual attestation as the New Testament'.

If you would like a fuller answer I suggest reading:

Why Trust the Bible? by Amy Orr-Ewing, IVP, Leicester, 2005

The New Testament Documents: Are They Reliable? by **FF Bruce, Downers Grove, IL: Inter-Varsity Press, 1981** – this is also available to read online at: *http://www.worldinvisible.com/library/ffbruce/ntdocrli/ntdocont.htm* (correct at time of printing).

Do you believe Jesus was born of a virgin?

The Bible clearly teaches that Jesus was indeed born of a virgin. Seven hundred years before the birth of Jesus, the prophet Isaiah prophesied saying, 'Therefore the Lord Himself will give you a sign: Behold a virgin shall conceive and bear a Son and shall call His name Immanuel …'[40] Matthew, the Gospel writer describing the birth of Jesus quotes this passage and adds the meaning of the word, 'Immanuel' saying, "which is translated, 'God with us.'"[41] Luke's Gospel also explicitly and repeatedly says that Mary was a virgin when she conceived, and tells how shocked both Mary and Joseph were upon receiving the news of Jesus' conception because they had not had sexual relations.

---

40.   Isaiah 7 v. 14

41.   Matthew 1 v. 23

Jesus was God taking on Himself humanity. He was fully God and fully human, and therefore it is natural that He should be born of the Holy Spirit and of Mary. It would be hard to understand how Jesus could be God if He was conceived of a human father and mother.

It is wrong though to think in terms of Mary as the 'mother of God'. The Bible never uses that phrase, and it is not true. She was blessed by God, and in her song, the Magnificat, confessed that she needed a Saviour as any human being does. Later, the Bible makes it clear[42] that she bore children in the normal way through sexual intercourse.

What good has Jesus done for the world?

It is hard to imagine our world if Jesus had not come. However, in the purposes and plan of God, it was never going to happen. God who is beyond time saw His Son Jesus as slain before the foundation of the world.[43] So in creating all things, God knew that we would rebel against Him, and that in the fullness of time Jesus would come to die and rise again as an atoning sacrifice for our sin. In His 33 years Jesus went about doing good. He

---

42. See Matthew 12 v. 46 – 50 and 13 v. 55 - 56

43. Revelation 13 v. 8

ministered to and met the needs of the people He met. He does the same today, on the basis of His finished work. He reconciles people to God, giving those who trust Him eternal life and the joy of living with Him through good and tough times.

The spin-offs from Jesus are themselves amazing. How different would be the architecture of the world, with no churches or cathedrals. The literature of our world would be much poorer. Books such as 'A Tale of Two Cities' by Charles Dickens, 'The Lion, the Witch and the Wardrobe' by CS Lewis, 'Uncle Tom's Cabin' by Harriet Beecher Stowe, with a host of others contain themes of one dying in place of another, or the impact of Jesus on the lives of people today. Their influence on society has been immense.

The music of the world would be unrecognizable if Jesus had not been born. Not only would we never have heard Handel's Messiah, Bach's 'Jesu, Joy of Man's Desiring' or Andrew Lloyd Webber's 'Jesus Christ Superstar', but we would have been bereft of thousands of hymns such as 'Amazing grace' and 'Abide with me'.

Art lovers of the world would find art galleries quite bare. So much of the world's art has concentrated on the birth, life, death and resurrection of Jesus. Holman Hunt's paintings 'The Light of the World' and 'The Shadow of the Cross' and Rembrant's 'The Return of the Prodigal Son' are some of the greatest works in the world. Sculptures of Jesus and His cross are scattered across the world, and not only in churches.

For two thousand years, multitudes of people have given their lives, often in far flung, difficult parts of the world, to serve and meet the needs of the poor and disadvantaged. Their motive has been their trust in Jesus and a desire to follow Him. Many of the great social reforms of our own land were led by people who had come to know God and as a result gave their energies to serving Him by alleviating the suffering of others.

However, I would want to stress that, most importantly, if Jesus had not come there would be no way for human beings to be forgiven for all their wrong. If Jesus had not come, we could not know peace with God; there would be no way of going to heaven.

However, Jesus was born. He did live. He died and rose again. The impact of His life has continued to grow, and His birthday is still the greatest celebration in our calendar.

Why did Jesus die on the cross?

The Bible says that every person has done wrong, with no exception. Even the old lady down the road, who makes cakes for the local church tea, always smiles and seems to do a good turn every second of the day, is sinful by God's holy reckoning! The Bible teaches that sin has gripped and affected us all.

God is a holy God – He is totally perfect, faultless, and without sin. His holiness is such that He cannot tolerate sin. He is of purer eyes than to look at it, but neither can he pretend it doesn't happen. The dilemma here is that sin cuts us off from God so that we do not have a relationship with Him – something He wants because He loves us.

It's for this reason that Jesus died. Because God is abounding in love for us, He sent His only Son, Jesus, to die bearing the penalty we deserve, in order to bring us back to Himself. Jesus died, the Righteous for the unrighteous, to bring us to God.

Why did God choose this method to rescue us? No human being has the answer to this. The Bible says that there cannot be forgiveness of sin without the shedding of blood. God sets the standards and we won't always plumb the depths of them. God has acted totally consistently with His character. We do know, however, that the sentence God requires has been paid on our behalf and we can go free, if we trust Him and receive Him. Let me ask you, 'Will you do this?'

How could Jesus die for me when I wasn't yet born?

Taking merely a cursory glance at this question leaves any answer seeming illogical making it easy to quickly dismiss what Jesus did that afternoon on a cross outside Jerusalem. However, if we look at the issue seriously for a moment longer we will see that actually what Jesus achieved was indeed for you and me.

Jesus is God, and because of His love for us He left the lofty heights of worship and adoration in heaven to come earth. He came to die – the only person who was born with that intention.

That begs the question as to why did He choose to come to earth if He knew He would die? He came because you and I need rescuing. God, unlike a human, doesn't just see today, or yesterday – He sees tomorrow too. In fact, more than just seeing the future, He knows the future. He knows what will happen tomorrow. Nothing takes God by surprise. God never holds an emergency committee meeting because something has happened which took Him by surprise. God has never said, "I didn't expect that!"

God is outside of and beyond time. God is not constrained by hours and days. He is the creator of all things including us. He knows us better than we know ourselves. He knows the sins which we have committed, and those that we have yet to do. So too, Jesus' death encompasses both yesterday, today and tomorrow. When Jesus died on the cross He bore the sin of the past, the present and the future. All our sin was future sin for Him, but He paid for it all when He died. His death is all sufficient, for all people, in all times, which includes you and me. For that, we can be eternally grateful.

If Jesus died for sin, why isn't everyone forgiven?

The cross is central to the good news of Jesus. That is why Christians often get so passionate about it. While Jesus was hanging on a rugged tree put into the shape of a cross, bleeding and dying, He wasn't just suffering physically, but spiritually too. He was taking upon Himself the sins of the world.

That is why the cross of Jesus is our only means of forgiveness. Because Jesus died, and rose from the dead, you and I have access to God!

God offers this forgiveness, rescue and restoration to everyone. He offers it to you! There is no other route. Jesus is the only way. That's why it's so important what you do with Him. Salvation is a free gift, offered to everyone, but like any gift, it has to be received or accepted before it becomes truly yours.

I recently bought a 48 box of Smarties for my grandsons, from one of those big wholesalers. When I took it home and told them I had a present for them they were, as ever, very excitable. I pulled the box of Smarties out of the bag. They could hardly believe their eyes; 48 tubes are almost too much for three little boys to comprehend.

Though I had bought the gift, told them about it, and even held it out and offered it to them, it wasn't truly theirs until they received and accepted it from me. At that point it was theirs and they could fully enjoy it and all its 'benefits'.

Jesus' death is a little like that. It is a gift we have to accept, not a reward we deserve. If a person rejects or neglects the gift of Jesus, then the responsibility of that choice is entirely his or hers. The Bible says the result of sin is death – but God's gift is eternal life.[44] The big question is, will you accept it?

Did Jesus really rise from the dead?

One of the main authors of the New Testament, Paul, said, 'if Jesus had not been raised our preaching is useless, and so is your faith'.[45] It's true; this is where Christianity stands or falls – the resurrection of the historical Jesus. It's amazing that the New Testament never tries to prove the resurrection, it assumes it. The first century person just believed it. Why? Because of the empty tomb – there is no way round it. There are six independent testimonies to it in the New Testament, and three of them are by eye witnesses.

The tomb where Jesus was buried, though guarded (by probably 16 Roman guards) was empty three days after Jesus was buried there. It is described in the Bible as being sealed, secure and set

---

44. Romans 6 v. 23

45. 1 Corinthians 15 v. 14

with a guard.[46] If Jesus did not rise, how do you account for the empty tomb? Here are a few ideas that people have suggested, and my replies to them:

Number 1: The disciples stole the body.

This is an interesting idea, and was first put about by the guards who were supposed to be guarding the tomb and the body. They were bribed to say that while they slept the disciples came and stole the body of Jesus.[47] First, soldiers would not dare to fall asleep on duty for they knew the bitter consequences if they were caught. But more importantly, if I was a barrister in a court of law I would want to ask them how they knew if they were asleep!

Perhaps more significantly though, I would want to ask why would they want to steal the body and then say Jesus was risen from the dead? To propagate a lie? Why did they all face torture and ultimately die for their belief if it was just a hoax? And how would they have stolen the body? Within hours of Jesus' death and burial they would have had to formulate a plan to get past the soldiers who were there protecting the body because the Jewish leaders had expressed fear that his body would be stolen. They then had to sneak past the soldiers, move a huge stone which was sealed to the grave, unwrap the dead body of Jesus, then carry His naked corpse away from the tomb to do what with it? No Jew would have carried the body, as that would render him ceremonially unclean. And where would they have put it?

No, these disciples were convinced that Jesus had risen from the dead.

Number 2: The authorities stole the body.

That would make more sense. Neither Roman nor Jewish leaders would have wanted any reminder of the significant life of Jesus or

---

46. Matthew 27 v. 66
47. Matthew 28 v. 13

the fact that they sent Him for crucifixion. But when Christianity was growing and they were doing everything they could to stop it, why not just produce the body, parade it prominently, and Christianity would have been crushed. They had no body to produce because they hadn't stolen it.

Number 3: The women went to the wrong tomb in their distress – it was a mistake caused by confusion.

Grief is a terrible thing. Nevertheless, we do read that the women who followed Jesus 'observed the tomb and how His body was laid' before 'they returned and prepared spices and fragrant oils'.[48] We know too, that where Jesus was buried was not in a graveyard but in a garden where there was a new tomb in which no one had yet been buried.[49] But the question remains whether they had still made a mistake. Then why didn't the authorities just go to the right tomb and produce the body when they wanted to stop the spread of Christianity? Also, it seems rather far fetched that all the other followers of Jesus also went to the wrong tomb. Further, the risen Jesus showed Himself alive and risen from the dead to literally hundreds of people before His ascension to heaven.

Number 4: Jesus didn't really die, but swooned into unconsciousness as He hung on the cross in such agony and trauma.

This theory is not a new one. It was first suggested by Venturini in the 16th century. But the argument is really saying that Jesus was beaten, nailed to a cross, declared dead by professional executioners, then had a spear put through His side from which came blood and water, was bound in spice-filled grave clothes, then buried in a sealed tomb. In this grave, He survived three days in a damp cave with no food or drink, revived, got out of His grave clothes, pushed a large rock door out of the way

---

48. Luke 23 v. 55 - 56

49. John 19 v. 41

(something which two physically fit people could not do), got past the armed guard protecting the grave, and then walked several miles on feet which had been impaled with nails.

No, there is no plausible objection to the resurrection, it is clearly historical. That is why when people carefully look at the evidence for the resurrection they become convinced that it really happened. It was prophesied in the Old Testament as well as repeatedly by Jesus. The risen Jesus was seen by hundreds of people. Frightened disciples were transformed into people who would go on the streets to proclaim Christ, and later lay down their lives because they were followers of Him. The resurrection of Jesus was recorded or referred to by Jewish and Roman historians, as well as Christians, and leaves Jesus accomplishing something which no other person has ever been able to do.

Section 4

Questions about Morality

What is sin?

There is no other book, internet article or blog that deals so thoroughly with the subject of sin as the Bible does. The good news is that the Bible also thoroughly explains the remedy for sin.

Sin is always serious, because it separates us from God who is holy and who cannot tolerate any sin. It brings God's guilty verdict on us. We were created to know God in a personal way, and yet our rejection of God, in breaking His commands, has cut us off from Him.

Sin is missing the mark, or falling short of God's requirements. It is a deviation from all that is right – an act of wilful disobedience to God. The Bible pictures sin in different ways:

It is like a burden too heavy for us to carry;
It is like a chain from which we cannot free ourselves;
It is like dirt we cannot wash off;
It is like a debt we owe God but can never pay;
It is like a disease for which we cannot find a cure.

Yet Jesus said of Himself, to a crowd of people to whom He was preaching, 'I want you to know that the Son of Man has authority on earth to forgive sins.'[50]

50.　Mark 2 v. 10

The pictures of sin above leave us in a dire state if we are left there. However, because Jesus takes upon Himself the sin of the world...

The burden can be removed;
The chain can be broken;
The dirt can be cleaned up;
The debt can been paid, and
the disease can be cured.

The way God describes our sin-filled life makes it look more like a rubbish dumb than a thing of beauty. Here is what the Bible says are some of the things on the dump...

'...sexual immorality, impurity, lustful pleasures, idolatry, sorcery, hostility, quarrelling, jealousy, outbursts of anger, selfish ambition, dissension, division, envy, drunkenness, wild parties, and other sins like these. Let me tell you again, as I have before, that anyone living that sort of life will not inherit the Kingdom of God.'[51]

This is serious stuff, isn't it? This is what God wants to clear up. We can't do it ourselves; we need God to step in.

When God begins to work in someone's life he or she begins to become aware that they are sinful in the sight of God. After all, He is holy; we are not. God diagnoses us as sinners, not to leave us condemned and written off, but so that He might cure us. He wants to take away guilt and give us new life in the Lord Jesus. The Bible says, '"Come now, let us reason together," says the Lord. "Though your sins are like scarlet, they shall be as white as snow; though they are red as crimson, they shall be like wool."'[52]

Sin is serious, and has consequences, but God calls us to come to Him, turn away from our sin and allow Him to forgive us, clean us and change us.

---

51.   Galatians 5 v. 19 - 21

52.   Isaiah 1 v. 18

Who decides what is right and wrong anyway?

There are those who argue that there is no absolute standard of right and wrong. So that what one may see as alright, another might see as wrong and vice versa. This is common post-modern thinking, but it doesn't work. Like it or not we live in a world of absolutes.

That's why we have Chartered Engineers and Surveyors. There are rules and guidelines that need to be followed when constructing a building to ensure that it is built correctly. They are not invented to spoil our fun of building crooked buildings that will be a danger to people. Of course not. These absolutes, these rules are made for our long term good and our safety.

It is the same with living. There are absolute standards laid down by God Himself.

Some time ago my son bought a wardrobe from IKEA. Being a typical male he charged on ahead without reading the instructions. It looked simple enough and he thought he could quickly knock it together. He would gladly admit he is no carpenter but this wasn't exactly a tough job. Two hours later, as he was struggling to find where the final pieces went, he presumed IKEA had made a mistake and included the wrong parts. It was then that he realised he had built the wardrobe back to front. How stupid he felt! Why didn't he follow the instruction sheet provided? Why didn't he do the obvious thing and follow the guidelines? It would have saved him time and a load of mess, and the stress level he experienced would not have been an issue.

Unfortunately, and more seriously, we humans do something

quite similar. We totally ignore the Creator's instructions, think we can go it alone, do our own thing, but end up in a whole heap of trouble.

God is the Creator of the universe. He brought it into being, and He sustains it. He has, therefore, every right to bring standards into the world that are irreplaceable and unchanging. Some of them we easily agree with: murder is wrong; as is paedophilia; but we then begin to struggle with a few that we want to call 'grey areas'. We want to challenge whether homosexual activity really is wrong. And we prefer to excuse a little lie.

We are soon on shaky ground, because we are leaving the Creator's instructions behind and, in effect, saying to Him, 'we know best'.

God made the world; God sustains the world; one day, God will judge the world. These things considered it is right and fair that God sets the standards. God rules according to His laws.

The trouble is we love sin too much. We enjoy doing wrong. That is why God the Father sent Jesus the Son to be the Saviour of the world.

Why all the fuss about homosexuality?

God created us, making us male and female. We were made to enjoy God and each other. He created us as social and sexual beings and, having done so He described His creation as 'very good'. Sex is a gift from God, given first that humans might, in an emotional and physical way, be able to express and give love, and secondly it is given for reproductive purposes.

Out of love for us, God has laid down and communicated to us the rules by which sex should be enjoyed, and beyond which sex becomes a selfish and godless act. There is nothing dirty about sex which is practised in the way that God intended. Rather it is an act of holiness fulfilling God's purposes for us.

The Bible teaches that sex is for a man and a woman who are committed to each other in a faithful married relationship. Any form of sex outside marriage is sin, and less than God's best.

Sexual practice between two people of the same sex is not what God intended, and is an abuse of the physical body and of the stewardship of sexual desire. It can never lead to reproduction, and very often leads to long-term unhappiness as one becomes immersed in the sub-culture of those practising it. It often leads to guilt and shame.

Some people going through puberty, experimenting with the new world of sexuality, go through a homosexual phase. That does not mean at all that they are homosexuals. There is no genetic evidence that some people are born homosexuals; although even if there was that does not mean it is right as we live in a world that has become far less than God created. Homosexual practice is a choice. It is often as a result of wounded sexuality or weak role models in childhood that a person finds their inclination towards the same sex. God will help any individual to honour Him in their sexuality, either by redirecting them to a heterosexual path, or receiving the strength to live a celibate life.

Section 5

Questions about suffering

Why doesn't God stop the trouble?

Something is wrong with our world. We know too much of wars, earthquakes and famine. The world has shed too much blood and so many tears. There has been more than enough abuse, injustice, loneliness, selfishness and despair. Disease and death come as uninvited guests to wreck our comfort zones and leave us questioning. We have grown tired of false hopes and promises, whether made by politicians, doctors, bosses or lovers. Life seems so unfair. Most of us are conscious that there is a God but why doesn't He act to stop it all? God's message to humanity, the Bible, tells us that He is all powerful and altogether loving, so we ask why does He not intervene?

I will answer this one big question, by answering ten more detailed questions:

1. Has the world always been a place of suffering?

We know from the Bible that when God created the world, everything was 'very good'. There was no suffering, sin, sorrow or death. The world as it was became the world as it is, after a deliberate act of rebellion against God. At the beginning of time, the first human beings chose to discover the knowledge of both good and evil, but as a result creation was wrecked and ruined. Death and corruption entered all that God had made.

2. Does that mean that if someone is suffering they must have done something bad?

The oldest book in the Bible (which has 66 books in all) is the Book of Job. It tells the story of how Job in just a few days lost his family, wealth and health. His friends tried to explain what was happening, but didn't know that the devil, Satan, the supreme cynic, had suggested to God that everyone has a price tag. It was Satan himself that took away from Job all that he had. At the end of the book God spoke and asked the characters of the book about sixty questions. They showed that we humans don't understand the power, works and ways of God as we like to think we do. Job was blessed by God again, but His troubles teach that it is a mistake to have glib answers to suffering. On this occasion it was the devil who directly caused his problems.

Before there was sin, there was no suffering, and sometimes when we do wrong today there are immediate consequences. Smoke cigarettes and it will ruin your lungs; drink too much alcohol and it will wreck your liver; drive too fast and who knows what will happen? But suffering is not necessarily a direct result of sin. Jesus said about a man born blind that it wasn't the result of his sin or his parents' sin that there was blindness, but God would bring great good from even the disability.

On another occasion, Jesus spoke about an incident where a tower had collapsed and killed eighteen people, and a dreadful time when a group of worshippers had been martyred by Pontius Pilate. Jesus then taught that the lesson to learn is that unless we turn to God and trust Him, we also will perish. We are bound up in the bundle of life, and sadly those whom we feel should not suffer, often do. It is part of the life which we live. Just as it is inevitable that flint stones knocked together cause a spark, so it seems certain that human beings suffer.

3. Isn't suffering pointless?

God can bring good even from bad circumstances. He is never taken by surprise, for He knows all things: past, present and future. God is love … always! In 1911 there was a dreadful mining disaster in Durham. The then bishop, during the Memorial Service in the beautiful, packed cathedral used a tapestry to illustrate his message. Showing the reverse side there was a tangled mess of embroidery thread that seemed meaningless. Then Bishop Moule turned over the tapestry to reveal, intricately woven, the words, 'GOD IS LOVE'. From our position life can seem deeply confusing, but God always works in love. He can bring good from even the worst situations of life.

Though we can never be glib, the suffering of some has often brought out love, compassion and care from others. A world where there was no hurt could easily become a horribly callous place.

For the people who know God in a personal way, they have the assurance that God never wastes any tears, or time, or toil, or pain. He uses everything, even suffering, in His great plan and purpose.

4. Could it be that when disasters happen, God is punishing people?

We know from the Bible that God does judge nations and people. God hates the wickedness that we so easily take for granted. It may be that suffering could bring a person or a nation to the point where they will repent, turn away from their sin, and turn back to God. It is not for human beings though, to say that such and such an incident is God's judgement. He knows, but we do not!

5. Why did God allow Jesus to suffer?

Jesus had done no wrong at all. He was Himself God, come down to earth to live as a man, and He went about doing good. He healed the sick, raised the dead, calmed the storm at sea, fed the hungry, and turned around messed up lives. And yet people crucified Him. It is hard to imagine a worse way to die: His back was beaten, and on it He was made to carry a rough Roman cross; His naked body was nailed to the cross on which He was lifted up to die; then God laid on Him the sin of the world – all sin, from the beginning to the end of time. Jesus was cut off from His friends, and even from His Father God, as He paid the penalty for our sin. The Bible says: 'All we like sheep have gone astray; we have turned every one to his own way, but the Lord has laid on Him (i.e. Jesus) the sin of us all'. 'Jesus was wounded for our transgressions' so that through all His suffering, God would be able to offer forgiveness to people like you and me. Jesus' darkness gives light to those who will trust Him. He died so that we could be reconciled to God. There was no other way whereby the judgement of God against sin and the love of God for us could be satisfied.

6. Will there ever be justice?

We also see from Jesus that death is not the end. He died on the cross, was buried, and then three days later rose from the dead. He had repeatedly spoken of life after death, of heaven and hell. Then He demonstrated the truth of this by rising from the dead. If this life is all that there is, so many people would have cause to be miserable. But there is more than just "three score years and ten".

In Psalm 73, written centuries before Jesus was born, the writer found the whole issue of suffering, and the fact that 'good' people often suffer most, led him to question his deep faith. That was until He began to see things from God's perspective and from eternity's point of view. Then he saw the shortness of life compared with the length of eternity, and realised that God would eventually right the wrongs, and justice would rule in every situation.

7. Can anyone really explain why some people suffer and others seem to be spared?

As human beings, we cannot understand why some have such a tough time, but others just sail through life. But what we know about God enables us to trust, and even be thankful for the things which are beyond us. We read in the Bible, 'The secret things belong to God, but the things revealed belong to us and to our children that we learn to obey all the works of the law'.[53]

God has revealed so much about Himself: His love, His justice, His holiness, and His coming to earth in the Lord Jesus. He has revealed things about us too: that we are made in His image; that we are given an eternal existence; that we can come to know God in a personal way, and that God knows what He is doing in our lives.

Yet there are things we just do not understand. Why does a young child die? Why is a young mother taken? Why a tsunami? Why was it that some people and not others were killed or maimed as a result of terrorism? Why the Taliban? Why cancer? This side of eternity will never provide the answers to individual stories of suffering, but we can rest in the character of God: He has not lost control of our world.

8. Why do some people get away with great wickedness?

So much suffering in the world has been caused by tyrants, terrorists, dictators and rulers. The bloodshed and tears poured out because of armchair rulers, who seem to be unable to see the world through eyes other than their own, is heart-rending. We are assured in the Bible that every individual, including kings and queens, presidents and prime ministers, will one day stand before God in judgement. They will have to give account for all that they have said and done. Justice will be served, and those

---

53.   Deuteronomy 29:29

who have rejected God will mourn over all that they did.

9. Will the world always be a place of suffering?

The Bible makes clear that the world as it is, will one day be destroyed, and God will make a new heaven and a new earth. This is described in some wonderful ways: a place where the lion will lie down with the lamb; where swords will be beaten and made into ploughs, where nations will speak peace to other nations, and there will be the sound of children playing on the streets with no fear of harm coming to them.

Not everyone will enjoy this new reign, though. For those who have rejected God's way of forgiveness, and reconciliation to Himself, there will be a place of endless suffering. It is too horrible to contemplate. Jesus lovingly warned about the reality of hell for those who reject Him. Yet God desires that no one should perish, but that all should truly repent and believe.

10. What should be my response to suffering?

God wants us to turn from what is wrong, and ask the once crucified, but now risen Jesus to forgive us, and live within us as Lord and Saviour. He promises that He will take us through life, through death and then to be with Him forever in heaven. Heaven is not a reward; it is a gift for those who will receive Jesus into their lives.

To trust Jesus like this does not mean that there will be no more suffering. Christians find that they are swimming against the tide of the world's thinking, and that can be hard. Nor does it mean that every question will be answered. Christians are always trying to find out more about the God they love because He first loved them and gave Himself for them. However, it does mean that we have a new relationship with the true and living God. We can rest in the certainty that He knows what He is doing even if we don't always understand why.

Isn't Christianity just a crutch for the weak?

This is a difficult question to answer in many ways. To some extent yes, it is, in other ways, no it isn't. Let me explain...

It is important to understand why people need Christianity, or to be more specific, why people need the man behind Christianity, namely Jesus. The Bible says, 'There is no one righteous, not even one; there is no one who understands, no one who seeks God. All have turned away, they have together become worthless; there is no one who does good, not even one.'[54] So if we have turned our backs on God, how does He see us now; what is His opinion of us?

When Jesus was on this earth He went for a meal with a group of people that were seen as the worst of the worst – people even called them "sinners" to their face. Because the religious leaders thought it was wrong for a man claiming to be God to dine with such people, they asked His disciples, '"Why does your teacher eat with tax collectors and 'sinners'?' Overhearing them Jesus replied, "It is not the healthy who need a doctor, but the sick. But go and learn what this means: 'I desire mercy, not sacrifice.' For I have not come to call the righteous, but sinners."'[55]

We are people with a sickness, a disease, that has infected everyone and we need to be healed, we need to be cured. Jesus is that cure, the only cure. So are Christians weak? Is Jesus a crutch for the lame? Yes, very much so. It is because we are sinners that we need a Saviour. 'It was our pains He carried -

---

54. Romans 3 v. 10 - 12

55. Matthew 9 v. 10 - 13

our disfigurements, all the things wrong with us. We thought He brought it on Himself, that God was punishing Him for His own failures. But it was our sins that did that to Him, that ripped and tore and crushed Him - our sins! He took the punishment, and that made us whole.'[56]

'For He will deliver the needy who cry out, the afflicted who have no one to help. He will take pity on the weak and the needy and save the needy from death. He will rescue them from oppression and violence, for precious is their blood in His sight.'[57]

Bearing all that in mind, how is it that the answer is complicated? The problem with the question is that it often comes from an assumption that Christians are flimsy, desperate loners with no hope in life. They join a church to make some friends and have something to do in their otherwise desolate and desperate lives. This simply isn't the case. Christians are very ordinary people from every walk of life who have come to know God in a very personal way, and that in itself makes us stronger and more daring than we could have imagined.

---

56. From Isaiah 53 v. 2 - 6 (The Message)

57. Psalm 72 v. 12 – 14

Section 6

Questions about religion

Don't all religions lead to God?

In recent years the educational system and media have taught that all religions do lead to God. Religions are presented as just different paths going up the same mountain, all leading to the same summit. Simple logic, as well as the Bible itself, makes it clear that this cannot be true.

Imagine you were drowning in the sea. You would not want people to stand on the shore and shout instructions about how to swim – especially if they were shouting over each other so that none of them could actually be heard. Worse still, if their instructions and advice were contradicting one another, the situation would be hopeless. However, if somebody dived in and rescued you, how delighted you would be! That's what you really need, not a list of instructions but a saviour – someone who is willing to jump into the water and risk their life at the cost of saving yours.

To put it very basically, all religions outside of Christianity are a list of "do's and don'ts". They aim to bring a person up to God. They are all about what we must do to save our lives, or reach heaven or its equivalent. True Christianity is different. Instead of us trying to reach to God, Christianity is about God coming to down to us. Jesus 'dived into the sea' to rescue us.

God is too big and holy for small, sinful people like us to try to reach Him. However, God took on Himself humanity, becoming a man, walking on this earth and dying to save us. God has come down to reach and rescue us.

The Bible says that '…at just the right time, when we were still powerless, Christ died for the ungodly…God demonstrates his own love for us in this: While we were still sinners, Christ died for us.'[58] That is the amazing truth of Christianity that sets it apart from all other religions, ideas, formulas or sects. It is not about what we have to achieve, but rather what God in Jesus has achieved for us. The fact that He died in order that we might escape the separation we have brought upon ourselves, and that He rose again, is totally different from any other religious teaching.

Only Jesus was pure and sinless. Only He could die to pay the price of sin. God says that there is only one remedy for the sin that is in this world, and that is that Someone should be able to act as our Substitute-Saviour. It sounds extreme – but sin is extreme; it sounds serious – but God takes it seriously. Thankfully, because of His great love for us, Jesus (the One who never did anything wrong) died for us (the ones in the wrong) to bring us to God.

So Jesus died to pay the sentence that was hanging over our heads, but He also came back from the dead. That's right – He died, and three days after dying He came out of His grave and was alive. It is another unique sequence of events in Jesus' life. Only Jesus rose from the dead.

There is great historical proof that Jesus rose from the dead. One can visit the graves of Mohammed, Buddha, Marx, the gurus, etc, but Jesus' grave is empty. Jesus is very much alive!

All religions do lead to God, in the sense that every individual will stand before God as judge. Every religion other than Christianity leads to God 'on the throne of judgement' whereas Jesus leads His people to God the Father 'on the throne of grace'. Jesus said

58.   Romans 5 v. 6 & 8

He was the only way to the Father (God), "I am the way, the truth and the life; no one comes to the Father but by Me."[59] Either He was and is an arrogant liar and we can ignore Him – or He is right and we should follow Him. Peter, Jesus' disciple added, "God has given no other name under heaven by which we must be saved."[60] The Apostle Paul wrote, "There is one God and one Mediator between God and men, the man Christ Jesus."[61] If we examine it, and are willing to swim against the prevailing tide, we will find that all the evidence shows Jesus is who He said He is and we should worship Him.

Isn't religion a matter of personal interpretation and sincerity?

Imagine for a moment you are suffering from a dreadful illness. In a hope to get better you drink something pink-looking from a bottle sincerely believing it to be medicine. In actual fact it is poison. Tragedy is certain to follow.

Sincerity can be a helpful thing, but truth is far more important than even being sincere. There is a difference between deciding what to believe and listing your favourite ten songs in order. One

59.   John 14 v. 6

60.   Acts 4 v. 12 (NLT)

61.   1 Timothy 2 v. 5

has an absolute answer, the other is subjective.

Jesus said, 'I am the way, the truth and the life. No one comes to the Father except through Me.'[62] Eternal life and eternal death are such important issues that we have to look beyond sincerity. We need truth.

With issues of this magnitude we must resist the danger of allowing personal feelings to keep us from the objective truth there is in Jesus. Faith in Him is not a question of taste and preference, but a matter of eternal significance. The notion 'That's okay for you but not for me' is clearly wrong here. It's not acceptable.

The issue of a relationship with God is absolutely crucial because mistakes have eternal consequences. It is vital, therefore, that our personal beliefs are correct.

Though there may be different interpretations concerning some less crucial teachings of the Bible, all the major truths are very clear to those who simply take on board what the Bible teaches. There are even summaries in the New Testament of its basic teaching, '…that Christ died for our sins according to the Scriptures, that he was buried, that he was raised on the third day according to the Scriptures, and that he appeared to Peter, and then to the Twelve.'[63] and, 'Here is a trustworthy saying that deserves full acceptance: Christ Jesus came into the world to save sinners - of whom I am the worst.'[64]

It is an abuse to try to change the emphasis of the Bible's teaching simply because what it says is unpalatable and cuts across our own beliefs. The truth of the Bible (God's Word) is plain to all who will honestly read it.

---

62. John 14 v. 6

63. 1 Corinthians 15 v. 3 - 4 (TNIV)

64. 1 Timothy 1 v. 15

Do you believe in reincarnation?

The eternal God clearly lays out the events that take place after our life on earth. In the later part of the Bible it reads, '...man is destined to die once, and after that to face judgment...'[65] Though we like to dream or imagine what life beyond the grave might be like, the wise and sensible approach is not to rely on fanciful wishes but on the knowledgeable God who created all things.

When on this earth, Jesus told a story of a rich man and a poor man called Lazarus. Both died. Lazarus believed and trusted in God (in fact that's what the name Lazarus means). Because of his faith he went to be with God in heaven. The rich man, however, showed his contempt for God by his lack of concern for his neighbour and was condemned to hell. There, in the most astonishing torment he lifted his eyes to heaven and begged for mercy, such was his agony. The answer came back, '...between us and you a great chasm has been fixed, so that those who want to go from here to you cannot, nor can anyone cross over from there to us.'[66]

What a person does with Jesus on earth matters for all eternity. When this earthly life is over there are no second chances, no re-runs permitted. Our good works do not rescue us, nor do they determine our fate. The Bible never teaches that there is a period of purgatory. Only through the death of Jesus are we saved and given heaven. We need to respond to His free offer of forgiveness – for this determines how we will spend eternity; rejecting Him leads to hell, like the rich man, but if we turn to and trust in Jesus,

---

65. Hebrews 9 v. 27

66. Luke 16 v. 26

we can be like the poor man, who went to be with God in Heaven. There is no middle ground, no fence to sit on.

What do you think about witchcraft, mediums and Ouija boards?

The Bible teaches that there is a devil. He is an angelic being created by God, probably long before our world was made. Satan, the devil, wanted God's throne. He was hungry for power and control, so led a rebellion against his Creator. He was cast of out of heaven, to hell, which was made by God for the devil and his angels. Jesus described what it was like when He said, 'I saw Satan fall like lightning from heaven.'[67]

Ever since, Satan's subtle device has been to try to make people imitators of him and turn against God. He has power, but not absolute power. He can do incredible things, but it is foolish to dabble with anything to do with Satan. As his banishment from heaven shows, he is doomed.

Early in the Bible God tells His people, 'Let no one be found

---

67.   Luke 10 v. 18

among you who sacrifices his son or daughter in the fire, who practices divination or sorcery, interprets omens, engages in witchcraft, or casts spells, or who is a medium or spiritualist or who consults the dead. Anyone who does these things is detestable to the Lord, and because of these detestable practices the Lord your God will drive out those nations before you.'[68]

Whether it is the Ouija board, a horoscope, fortune telling, tarot cards, or palm reading, God forbids it. This isn't because He is against us, but because He loves us and wants the very best for us. Would He die for us if this was not true? He wants to protect us from the things and beings that might harm us, even if they appear at first, innocent and fun.

A person can know fullness of joy and peace through knowing God. Jesus, though tempted by Satan himself, resisted the devil's empty offers of pleasure, lived, died and was resurrected, so that we too might be able to resist the devil today.

One day the devil will be bound, and his deceit and trickery will be over. The Bible says he will face horrific judgment and never be able to escape.[69]

Take God's advice and avoid all things to do with the devil, or contacting the dead. It's extremely dangerous and, as the example of Satan proves, leads to separation from God.

If you have already been involved, I encourage you to turn from these things, ask that the blood of the Lord Jesus will cleanse you from all sin, and that God's Holy Spirit will come to live within you. There is a dramatic incident of this happening in the days of the early church, which culminated in the new Christians burning a vast number of books about the magic arts.[70]

---

68. Deuteronomy 18 v. 10 - 12

69. See the description in Revelation 20 v. 2, 3 & 10

70. Acts 19 v. 11 - 19

Haven't wars been caused by religion?

The cause of war is on all occasions due to the sinfulness, greed and weakness of humanity. Some wars were started to bring about peace, others to gain, keep or regain power and territory. Others are simply a struggle to advance a leader's ego.

Sadly, there have been religious wars. Some religions even believe it is legitimate and right to fight to spread their cause. This is not the case with Christianity. Jesus told his followers to 'turn the other cheek' and later when one of them (Peter) failed to do this and cut off someone's ear with a sword, Jesus healed the injured person before commanding Peter to put away his sword. One of Jesus' titles is the Prince of Peace.

Therefore, when wars have been fought in the name of Jesus the perpetrators have been wrong and misguided. When someone fights in the name of Jesus it is like someone carrying out a crime in your name when you have specifically commanded him not to do so. It would not be fair to blame you for that crime, nor to blame wars on Jesus, even if they have been fought in His name.

Politics and religion stir strong feelings, but someone trusting in and obeying the instructions of Jesus will find that He calms aggression and gives a genuine concern and compassion to all. Jesus commanded Christians to love the people around us to the same degree that they love themselves. He commands us to love our enemies. These are not impossible instructions, for He assures us that He will give us all the help we need in order to obey.

Do you believe in miracles?

I certainly do! And if there was space I could tell you of the many that have happened in my life. Some may say that these miracles are just marvellous coincidences, that are simply freaky events that work out in our favour, but I am certain that God is behind them, and this is why…

It is a delightful, though sometimes a tough, discipline of mine to try and spend time each day with God. I do this by reading His Word, the Bible, and talking with Him through prayer. By reading the Bible He teaches me about His character and His work. Time and time again I have found that God has wonderfully answered my prayers. When I don't speak to God about the issues of my life, and the things on my heart, these amazing 'coincidences' seem to stop! It is very clearly God who is orchestrating these events.

The greatest miracle for me was when I trusted Jesus as my Lord and Saviour. He completely and irreversibly changed me. Since then I have met people who have perhaps had an even more dramatic turn around in their life. For example, I have seen a friend, who was an alcoholic and a drunk, become sober; a car robbing thief become a man who is now honest, gentle and kind; another friend was immoral and now has become pure and faithful; while another had a foul and abusive mouth – she now speaks in such a kind and supportive way. This change doesn't just happen by will power. It comes through the miraculous work of God in a person's life.

A while ago I received a letter from a prisoner who had not long before become a real Christian. This is what he wrote to me.

'The jury pronounced me 'Guilty' and the judge sentenced me; now I have felt God pronounce me 'Forgiven' and that my sentence has been paid, through the blood of Jesus.'

If that is not a miracle I don't know what is!

God is not a psychological prop, but the miracle-working God who can change you today if you trust Him.

Some people though want more. In fact, even as Jesus walked this earth the leaders of the day asked Him for more signs and miracles. However, Jesus warned them that it was not the right demand to make.[71]

Some people want to be healed, or for their lottery numbers to come up, before they will trust in God. They want a sign. Instead, God calls us to come to Him now, sign or no sign, for He is the all-knowing, all-forgiving God who knows what is best for us.

---

71. You can read about this in Matthew 12 v. 38 - 40

Section 7

Questions about life after death

Don't the good go up (to heaven) and the bad go down (to hell)?

There is a fundamental problem with this question. Quite simply it is that assumption that there are good people in this world!

I wonder how you make your judgements about who is good and who is not. Is Nelson Mandela good in your mind? What about the charity worker labouring in Bangladesh? Perhaps it's the local Neighbourhood Watch co-ordinator who is good in your eyes? Are you and I good ... all the time?

The Bible answers those questions very starkly: 'There is no one who always does what is right, not even one. There is no one who understands. There is no one who looks to God for help. All have turned away. Together, everyone has become useless. There is no one who does anything good; there is not even one.'[72] While from time to time we may do kind things, that doesn't make us good. Again, the Bible teaches that we have all been infected by sin, which spoils every area of our life.

It is for this reason that God has to punish us for our wrongdoing. It is palatable to say that heaven is a real place but we find it less comfortable to believe that hell, too, is real, where real people exist, experiencing real judgement for personal sins committed.

---

72.   Romans 3 v. 10 - 12

The Bible says that we will all stand in the dock before God in judgement. God makes a judgement on each of our lives and the problem is we all fall short of His standard, because it is perfect.

The great news of the Bible is that God came to rescue us from what we deserve so that we may be rescued and brought from death and darkness (hell) into His wonderful light and life (heaven).

Surely, when you die, that's it?

There's a quirky song in Yorkshire called, 'On Ilkley Moor bah t'at'. Perhaps you've heard of it. It describes a man dying after walking on the Moor without his hat! He's buried, eaten by worms, the worms eaten by ducks, and then us eating the ducks! The final verse starts with the line, 'Then we will all have eaten thee…'

Alright, it's slightly bizarre and a bit of fun, but on a serious note change and decay affects us all; our bodies will one day die and decompose. Was Bertrand Russell right, though, when he said 'When I die I rot'? The Bible teaches that that view is profoundly wrong. We are not just bodies, but have an eternal existence.

When someone says something that 'hurts' you, it is not your body they have hurt, but your feelings, the real, inner you. The Bible teaches that each of us has a soul and a spirit, and that it is the soul that they have hurt. The Bible insists that the soul and spirit live forever. That is why the Bible can say, '...people are destined to die once and after that face judgement...'[73] The Bible states that when our earthly body dies that is not the end; the real us will continue eternally.

Some people say, 'But no-one has ever come back from the dead to tell us about it.' Of course, this is not true – Jesus did that very thing. Jesus died, and rose again, and when He did He spoke of heaven and warned of hell.

How could a God of love send people to hell?

This question is a big issue, especially when one begins to understand just how great is God's patience and love toward us. I wonder whether we need to turn the question around and say how can a God of love *not* send people to hell?

Before we do that, however, it is important to ask another

---

73.   Hebrews 9 v. 27a

question? Why do we say God is a God of love? Where have we learnt that, or what has made us come to that conclusion? It is right to describe our Maker as a 'God of love' for the Bible teaches and demonstrates this repeatedly. It is because of His great love that Jesus died for us when we were still turning our back on Him.

However, the point to be made is this, if we are confident enough to accept one of the Bible's teachings (that God is a God of love) why are we not willing to take on board other topics of its teaching, namely that Hell is real and that those who reject God are determining their own lost eternity? Can we pick and choose from the doctrines of the Bible? It's a dangerous game to play, that only leads us away from the complete truth that God has revealed.

On 16th April 2007 the world's media zoomed its 'lens' on the Virginia Polytechnic Institute and State University (Virginia Tech) in Blacksburg, Virginia. At 7.15am on that crisp Monday morning, a student named Seung-Hui Cho began one of two attacks that killed 32 of his peers and injured 23 others. After the second attack was complete he turned the gun upon himself and committed suicide.

Cho never stood trial for the vulgar crimes he committed. He never 'had his day in court'. Justice had no chance to fall upon this man. In many ways he 'escaped'. Three years later a similar event unfolded in Whitehaven in Cumbria when Derek Bird murdered thirteen people before taking his own life. Again, he could not be brought to trial. But is that fair? Is it just? We innately know that it is far from just. Do we not cry out for our loving God to punish wickedness? Something within us longs for justice.

The problem comes when we look at the issue of where to distinguish who deserves what. Compared to Cho and others, you and I may look like earthly saints, but this is not the standard that God sets for judgement. God doesn't compare us like for like – He Himself is the standard of righteousness. We can neither attain nor maintain this altogether impeccable standard. The Bible says that no one is good, no one meets God's perfect standard, and no one is without sin.

This leaves us in the same vulnerable position as Cho. The God of love cannot simply ignore our sin, however 'small' we may consider it to be. Part of God's character is to be just, totally and utterly. However, equally part of His nature is to love. It is on the cross where Jesus died that these two characteristics come together with equal power. Because of His justice a penalty had to be paid for our sin, which was death; because of His love for us, Jesus paid the sentence on our behalf in order that we might be rescued and go free. What love! The question is how will we respond? Will we just reject what Jesus did, reject His love and face the horrific eternal consequences, or will we gratefully accept the amazing rescue provided through Jesus?

What happens to someone who commits suicide – do they go to hell?

To commit suicide is to do something that God has specifically told us is wrong. It is breaking the sixth commandment which is, 'You shall not murder'.

Perhaps it is because some films, songs, or websites give the impression suicide is a way of escape and a means of proving one's significance, that it has been made to seem a possible option when difficulties arise. Sadly, in some cases this has led to others copying their actions, leading to further tragedy.

Suicide is not a Christian response to difficulties or unhappiness. Characters in the Bible who asked God to take their lives from them always had their prayer refused, because God had further work for them to do, for Him and for others.

I, personally, have struggled for a number of years with depression. I cannot explain it, but at times it has been horrendous. I have on numerous occasions had to battle with the temptation of suicide, and so I don't approach this subject lightly. Suicide is a selfish act, however, which leaves a wake of guilt, regret and grief to those who are left behind. In fact, it transfers all one's own pain on to those who remain.[74]

So does this make suicide an unforgivable act, especially considering that it is the last thing one does – and leaves no chance to ask for forgiveness, or show remorse?

No. Suicide is like all other sin. While suicide has lasting, devastating consequences, God is big enough to forgive these actions. There are, I think, six accounts of suicide in the Bible, the most notorious being those of King Saul and Judas. Others are Abimelech, Samson, Ahithophel, and Zimri. As far as I can tell, none of the six is explicitly condemned for taking his life.[75] If someone is trusting in God, as their Lord and Saviour, this is a timeless forgiveness whatever their last action, be it an impure thought, an unkind word, or the taking of one's life. Because a

---

74. If this question is for you not merely academic but deeply personal, I would urge you to talk to a Church minister, vicar or pastor. Don't let what you consider to be shame keep you from being helped.

75. For further reading see, Good Question: Is Suicide Unforgivable? By Lewis B Smedes Christianity Today, July 10 2000, Vol 44, No. 8

Christian is forgiven he or she can have full assurance that this means all their guilt is no longer held against them. However, if someone is living with God ruling their life, it also means that they are told, and should desire, to avoid at all costs doing wrong against God – and this therefore includes suicide. Is suicide wrong? Yes. Is it unforgiveable? No.

What about the people who have never heard the Christian message?

First and foremost, it is essential that we ensure that we ourselves have responded to the good news of Jesus before we begin to be concerned about others.

There are several characteristics of God that give us insight to answer this question. We know He is a loving God, and it is for that reason He sent Jesus to be our Saviour. We also know that He is just and cannot simply ignore our sin, and because He is holy He cannot tolerate it either. As well, we know that He desires that no one will die without His rescue. These attributes of God give us the ability to answer this question with confidence, and say with Scripture, '...since the creation of the world God's invisible qualities - His eternal power and divine nature - have been clearly seen, being understood from what has been made, so that men are without excuse.'[76]

The Bible says that the creation alone gives enough evidence that there is a God who is the creator and sustainer of the world, a God of order and love. That is why in the Psalms in the Bible we read, 'The heavens declare the glory of God; the skies proclaim the work of his hands. Day after day they pour forth speech; night after night they display knowledge. There is no speech or language where their voice is not heard.'[77]

Each one of us has within us the sense of right and wrong (that is why we feel guilt), and an awareness that there is a God (that is why we pray when in need). People have to suppress this before they can deny His existence. Those who know little more about God than that will be judged with fairness and justice, consistent with His character. Longing for everyone to come to Christ, Christians have always been people who have been enthusiastic to share the good news of Jesus with others.

As I wrote at the start of this answer, the most important issue is that we, who have the opportunity to investigate, know and trust God must do so while we can.

---

76.   Romans 1 v. 20

77.   Psalm 19 v. 1 - 3

How will the world end?

The Bible is very clear that the world will not come to an end by a nuclear bomb, a collision with another planet, or even a catastrophic natural disaster, such as portrayed in the film, The Day After Tomorrow. Instead we are told that the end will come only at the time God chooses.

When Jesus first came to this world He came as a baby, laid in an animal trough. At the conclusion of the world He will come again, this time not as a baby, but as King of all the kings in the world and Lord of all. The Bible says that everyone will bow down to worship Him the moment He returns. He will rule the world in righteousness and have His rightful place in creation and in the minds of men and women.

Nobody knows the exact date and time of His return, but Jesus described how the world would be immediately before His return. So we can look for and recognise the signs and eagerly await His return. In Matthew's account of Jesus' life there is detailed teaching about the world as it will be before His return. The Book of Revelation further describes the turmoil that the world will witness before the momentous event when Christ comes to reign. In John's Gospel, we read how Jesus comforted His followers saying that He was returning to heaven to prepare a place for them, and all who put their trust in Him.

This is how the Apostle Paul describes what will happen when Jesus returns to this world: 'We tell you this directly from the Lord: We who are still living when the Lord returns will not meet him ahead of those who have died. For the Lord Himself will come down from heaven with a commanding shout, with the voice of the archangel, and with the trumpet call of God. First, the Christians who have died will rise from their graves. Then, together with them, we who are still alive and remain on the earth will be caught up in the clouds to meet the Lord in the air. Then we will be with the Lord forever.'[78]

For millions who have rejected the Lord Jesus, His return will be a time of immense regret and distress. If you are trusting in Jesus for the forgiveness of your sins then you can, with confidence, be looking forward to the bodily return of Jesus. It seems that so many of the signs of His imminent return have happened, and we must be ready for His return.

---

78.   1 Thessalonians 4 v. 15 - 17 (NLT)

Section 8

Questions about church

Can a person be a Christian and not go to church?

This question is of the same genre as 'Can a person be married and never see their husband or wife?' Well of course, legally, the answer is that they can. They have a piece of paper that says they're married and maybe a ring on their finger – they are legally married. However, that is not what marriage is all about. Marriage isn't about ticking a box. It's about a relationship. It's about enjoying time together, delighting in each other's company and sharing everything.

So, can a person be a Christian and not go to church? Well, yes. Though there seems to be something very incongruous if that happens. Going to church doesn't make a person a Christian, just as going to a garage doesn't make you a car. Christians go to church to worship God, to celebrate what He has done for them, to learn about Him, talk with Him and be encouraged by spending time with others who have trusted in Him as their Lord and Saviour.

God loves us and wants us to have a relationship with Him. If we have fully understood who He is and what He has done surely we will want that too, and one of the ways we can enjoy God is by going to church.

Aren't churches full of hypocrites?

I am sure there are many hypocrites in and out of churches. Hypocrisy is one of the many sins of which we humans are guilty and for which we need forgiveness. And every Christian who has found that forgiveness in Jesus will be conscious that they are not as Christ-like as they would wish to be. They will want to live consistent Christian lives, but when they fail they could well be accused of hypocrisy. Church, though, is welcoming to all. If you know you are a sinner, it is the place for you!

It seems greater hypocrisy to live without any thought of God, but then expect the church to give you the blessing of a Christian funeral when you have gone!

Why are there scandals in the church?

When we talk of 'the church', sadly we are usually referring to a system devised by humans, not all of whom have truly repented of sin and put their trust in Jesus. If Christ is not truly their Lord, and the Bible is not their guide, there will be issues which are seen as hypocritical and un-Christian. As in any organisation there are going to be scandals because every individual is flawed and, as in a computer programme, sin acts like a virus in the whole set up.

When the Bible speaks of the church, it is referring to the body of true believers, who are trusting Jesus, seeking to follow and serve Him in the Christian community of the church. Sadly though, they too will fail. A Christian is a sinner, who should be living in such a way that sin has become abhorrent to him or her. Every Christian still has a nature which does wrong, and sometimes sin comes to the fore. It has been like this since the beginning. Jesus warned about these things in His teaching, and many of the little books in our New Testament are letters written to churches to sort out errors in belief or behaviour.

I liken the church to a hospital, not a showroom. There is going to be mess, but God still meets with His people as they gather together. I spend a fair amount of time in churches, and despite heart-breaking times, generally speaking, I have found them to be places of immense love, care and refreshment.

Section 9

Questions about becoming and being a Christian

Can't I just live a good life to be OK with God?

Some believe that when we die, getting into heaven will be dependent upon a sort of weighing of our good deeds against our bad, and most reckon that, actually, they're pretty good.

But first: what does it mean to be good? We argue that if we haven't done anything desperately wrong, and we're not a murderer or a paedophile, then surely we're OK with God? The Bible teaches differently. We will be judged by God's standards, not our own. God is perfect – He has never done anything wrong because He is so pure and holy. His character is the standard of perfection. Being honest with ourselves we know that all of us have fallen short of this standard. We have all done things that we know are wrong, however insignificant they may seem to us.

The Apostle Paul, who penned the book of Romans, concluded, 'all have sinned and fall short of the glory of God'[79]. Let us not compare ourselves with each other, but rather with God.

Secondly, we are aware that we are not the people we should be. We all feel guilty for some things we have done. We know we haven't met our standards of morality in life, let alone God's standards. Looking at Jesus' summary of God's commands leaves us all condemned: 'Love God with all your heart, mind,

---

79.   Romans 3 v. 23

soul and strength ... and love your neighbour as yourself.'[80] We know we do not do these things. The definition of 'neighbour' according to Jesus is literally everyone, including our enemies. Compared to a perfect God we don't do well.

Thirdly, to God morality isn't the ultimate standard. According to the Bible, it is our response to God.

God created the world and us. He gives us life, but we ignore Him. That is the worst disobedience. We don't put God as number one in our lives. He is often not even a footnote in our short existence.

The Bible does not leave us to wallow in our own godless state. Instead, it teaches that God loved us so much that He sent Jesus, who lived a perfect life, went around doing good, but then who died on the cross to take our punishment for the wrong of which we are each guilty. We don't need to try to be good enough. We will never be good enough. We cannot become right with God by ourselves – we have to rely on the only thing that is sufficient to cover our sins – the forgiveness that is offered by Jesus, through His death on the cross. We neglect it at our peril.

---

80.   Mark 12 v. 30 - 31

Doesn't Christianity take away my freedom?

I saw a tee shirt with the words 'Freedom from the future'. It is an interesting thought but, of course, total nonsense! We each have commitments and responsibilities which mean that we can never be completely free. Freedom to choose and to act as we wish is not always good. For example, is it acceptable and fair that a paedophile has freedom to act as he or she wishes, even at the expense of another? Of course that could never be right. Or again, consider the drug dealers? Should they be free to supply no matter what the cost is to others? Nobody but a hardened criminal would think so.

Liberty is a great thing. I have worked in areas of the world where freedom of conscience is not permitted, so that religion or dissent is suppressed. It is a very oppressive atmosphere in which to live. What is true in nations is true for individuals. There is no one so bound as those whose rules for life are not God's. However, individual liberty should not be seen as just a licence to be selfish. Real freedom is not doing as we please, but having the power to do what is right.

The Bible teaches that all of us have a common problem, which the Bible calls sin. It's not a welcome topic of conversation and sometimes gives the impression that Christians are all about doom, gloom and judging other people. This is hardly the case.

Another misconception is that Christianity is about rules and regulations. Again, this is not true. God sets out commands which He calls us to follow. Ultimately, He calls us to love Him, and to love others. He does this because, when we do, we not only honour Him, but we also find that we too experience real pleasure which is elusive to people who never turn to Jesus.

No man was or ever has been as free as Jesus. He could do all things. He was free from greed, sham, spin and hypocrisy; He had no fear of skeletons in His closet – He had none. He had a great sense of duty, but that did not thwart His personality. Obedience to His Father's will didn't stifle Him, or undermine His freedom. True freedom is found in God. Jesus Himself claimed this when He said, 'I have come that you might have life and life in all its fullness.'[81] He is the source of life, the life-giver. And when you know Jesus and His freedom you are free to the maximum. In Jesus you become the person He created you to be, and in that you can be free to be yourself.

Can I repent on my deathbed?

Yes. There is a most wonderful example of this. While not quite on his death bed one of the criminals crucified with Jesus turned to Him saying, "Lord, remember me when you come into your kingdom" and Jesus spoke to him with the wonderfully assuring words, "I say to you, today you will be with me in Paradise." Heaven is not a reward, it is a gift, so anyone who genuinely repents and believes will be saved.

81.　John 10 v. 10

However, none of us know the day of our death. It's not only old people who die. We do not all have warning; some people die very suddenly. We can repent the day before we die, but as we do not know the day of our death, the best time to repent is *now*. The Bible always urges us to get right with God *today*.

Please spell out for me, how do I actually become a Christian?

Becoming a Christian, or coming to Jesus as Lord and Saviour, is so simple that even a child can do it and yet, sadly, so many make it harder than it needs to be and therefore miss the chance to be rescued and saved.

No-one is born a Christian; it is not something inherited, passed down, or earned. Instead, the Bible says, 'If you confess with your mouth that Jesus is Lord, and believe in your heart that God has raised Him from the dead, you will be saved.'[82]

My son went to hospital for an operation a while ago. When he did so he had to believe in, or have faith in, the anaesthetist, the surgeon and nurses, that they would take care of him.

---

82.   Romans 10 v. 9

With my work I do a fair bit of travelling and sometimes need to catch a plane over to Northern Ireland or further. When I do, I put my trust in the plane, the pilots and the crew. I believe they know what they are doing and will direct the plane (and me) safely to where I want to go. Believing in Jesus is similar. Becoming a Christian is a case of putting your full and total trust in God to forgive, save and change you.

Though being a Christian means enjoying a relationship with God, it is founded on certain definite beliefs. It is not possible to know God without believing what He says about Himself and us in His Word, the Bible. In believing, there are steps to finding peace with God:

First, be honest with God. Admit that you have rebelled against Him and not given Him His right place in your life. This is obvious; we know we're guilty, but our sin is more serious than we usually understand.

Secondly, believe that Jesus died on the cross to pay for your sin. God loved the world so much that He sent Jesus to die in our place. His death on the cross was not a mistake; it was planned – for us. What Jesus accomplished on the cross is enough to make us right with God and set us free.

Thirdly, repent. That is, to do a U-turn from living your own way and to start living God's way. God gives us His Spirit to help us change. We can't do this in our own strength. Instead, the God who created the earth, who came to be born in a manger, who walked on water, who fed the hungry, and healed the sick – the all-powerful God, is powerful in our lives as He changes us from the inside by His Spirit.

Fourthly, as you ask for forgiveness, commit your life to Him. You no longer have to live as an enemy of God, you can live as life is intended to be, which is, living life to the full with God at the centre. Romans chapter 10 verse 13 promises, 'anyone who calls on the name of the Lord will be saved' – this can be you.

Many have found that praying a prayer similar to the one below has helped them put their trust in Jesus:

'God, I admit I have done wrong in your sight. I have sinned and I am sorry. I want to turn from it. I believe that Jesus died on the cross to carry my sin and offer me forgiveness. Thank you that He rose again and gives me hope for eternity. Please transform and change me so that I can live your way each day. Thank you for hearing this prayer which I pray in the name of Jesus. Amen'

How should a Christian live?

One of the most memorable and iconic sound bites at the start of this twenty-first century will no doubt be the line from Barack Obama's victory speech in the light of his 2009 election win, in which he powerfully and triumphantly proclaimed, 'Change has come to America.'

Whatever you think of Obama, his policies and practices, what a spine-tingling occasion that was! And yet, despite their greatest desires, politicians and policies can never bring real, lasting change.

Real change, the Bible teaches, comes only when a person accepts Jesus as Lord and King of their life. Change comes from the inside, not simply through external cosmetic changes.

It is at that moment that a person enters into a wonderful relationship with the true and living God. This new friendship with God needs to be cultivated and deepened. Therefore a key part of the Christian life is to spend time growing in the knowledge of God. This is done by reading the Bible, His word, through which God communicates to us. It also includes spending time with other Christians who have a similar desire to know, understand and apply the Bible and worship Him. This is His church: a group of believers who meet for this purpose.

Like a person who has received some good news, you'll want to tell everyone about it. As I have said before in this book, my job takes me on the road for most of the year. Therefore my relationship with my wife, children and grandchildren is often via my mobile phone. When I receive good news I dial their number and excitedly tell them. That's what you do with good news – and the real, changed Christian is like that with the good news of Jesus. They just won't be able to keep it to themselves. Those who saw and heard Jesus' teachings said at the time, 'For we cannot help speaking about what we have seen and heard.'[83] Christians today should feel the same.

---

83.   Acts 4 v. 20

If I become a Christian how could I keep up the lifestyle?

The bad news is you can't 'keep up that lifestyle'. The Bible says each one of us is naturally bad all the way through, like a rotten fruit, an apple that's gone off and is diseased to the core.

The good news is that the Christian life isn't about us, and what we can do to improve. Instead it's about what Jesus has done and what the Holy Spirit does inside us.

God never leaves or forgets someone who is trusting in Jesus. The Bible says that a Christian is a 'child of God'. He promises to help us and gives us the strength and ability to be the people we ought to be.

A Christian is well aware that they are not always the person God wants them to be, but the forgiveness which comes through Jesus' death on the cross was for sin – past, present, and future.

The Christian life is a series of new beginnings. We should no longer love doing wrong and indulge in it. However, when as Christians we do wrong, we can have confidence that 'we have an advocate with the Father, Jesus the Righteous One.'[84] He will wash us from all our stains and help us as we press on with Him.

As a Christian trusts and obeys God, he receives real and lasting joy. God has saved us, and will keep us until we either leave this earth or Jesus returns.

---

84.   1 John 2 v. 1

Section 10

My question to you

My question to you

I have, at one time or another, been asked all the questions found in this book, at different times and in different ways, all by inquisitive minds.

Unfortunately, but out of necessity, most of the answers have been brief rather than thorough, exhaustive arguments. As we come to the end of this book I would like to ask you, the reader, a question. Here it is: who do you say Jesus is?

Perhaps it is that very question that got you thinking in the first place, and so you picked up this book to find out more. However, many people today haven't given the time the question justifies.

As a joke one night Sir Arthur Conan Doyle, the creator of Sherlock Holmes, sent a telegram to twelve of the most respectable men in London – 'Flee. All Is Revealed'. Within 24 hours six of them had made plans to leave the country.

We all have dark rooms in our lives; things we wish could be forgiven. We also wonder whether there is more to life than this. Why are we here? What's it all about? And you may wonder what Jesus has to do with it all anyway?

There is something amiss in the world and our lives. There is an awareness of more than we can see or touch. Jesus is the answer to life's big questions. The Gospel of John – one of the four accounts of the life of Jesus found in the New Testament - tells us of a meeting Jesus had with a religious leader called Nicodemus. Nicodemus was a good man, a really devout man and a member of the Jewish Ruling Council. He was very important and respected in matters of religion. If ever there was a man who seemed not to need a religious conversion – it was Nicodemus. But something happened to him. He heard about Jesus, His teachings and miraculous works. When Nicodemus came to Jesus he had similar questions on his mind, as we do twenty centuries later: is there more to life than this and what does Jesus have to do with it?

Jesus' reply is for everyone. Whether you are religious or not, respectable or not, it doesn't really matter for the moment. Jesus said simply, "Unless you are born again, you can never see the Kingdom of God."[85]

Don't be put off by the phrase with ideas of 'born again' meaning tele-evangelists or happy-clappy enthusiasts. Jesus is talking about the new life which can be ours as we are born from above and receive spiritual life. It is simply a description of someone becoming a Christian. You see, according to the Bible, we are not in a right relationship with God – in fact we live against Him. We are spiritually dead! Physically we can move and breathe, but in our relationship with God there is no life. We need to be given life, but how do we get it?

Jesus helped Nicodemus to understand the answer by referring to the early part of the Bible. It was a time when God's special people, the Israelites, were rebelling against God and everything was going wrong. In fact, their camp was infested with venomous snakes and people were beginning to die. They cried out to God and He answered them. He told them to make a bronze snake and put it at the centre of the camp so that whoever looked at it

85. See John 3

would be saved. If it appeared crazy what did they have to lose, so they did as they were commanded. They looked at it and they were saved.

Jesus told Nicodemus that this was a picture of His life and work. Jesus said, "Just as Moses lifted up the snake in the desert, so I must be lifted up, that everyone who believes in me will have eternal life'.[86]

Jesus came to be lifted up, to die on a cross – that was His life's mission. Death and disaster, guilt and loneliness: they are a result of living against God. But just as He gave the Israelites a way out, He gives us one too. Jesus died on the cross an innocent man. He did it as a substitute for us. We deserve punishment for our rebellion, but Jesus took it in our place. There is nothing we can do to make ourselves alive spiritually, but Jesus will give us new life. We can be born again.

Jesus summed it up perfectly in one of the most famous quotes in the world, whose reference John 3:16 can be seen sometimes placarded at sporting fixtures: 'For God loved the world so much that he gave his only begotten Son, so that whoever believes in him will not perish but have eternal life.'

Jesus, as He walked this earth, claimed to be God in human form, the Saviour of the world and the only way to God the Father. A few would say He is mad, others think He's deluded, but who do you say He is?

If you believe He is who He claimed to be, I urge you to trust Him as your Lord, your Saviour and your Friend. And do it today.

---

86.   See John 3

Do you want to know more?

Then please go to my web-site: *www.tell-me-more.org* or write to me care of the publishers.

10Publishing is the publishing house of 10ofThose. It is committed to producing quality Christian resources that are Biblical and accessible.

www.10ofthose.com is our online retail arm selling 1000s of quality books at discounted prices. We also service many church bookstalls around the UK and can help your church to set up a bookstall. Single and bulk purchases welcome. For more information contact: sales@10ofthose.com or check out the website.

www.10ofthose.com